Political Correctness

Exposed

*A Piranha
In Your Bathtub*

Marvin Sprouse

Be Blessed!

*Marvin & Charlene
& John*

Political Correctness
Exposed

A Piranha In Your Bathtub

Marvin Sprouse

STARBURST PUBLISHERS
™

P.O. Box 4123, Lancaster, Pennsylvania 17604

To schedule Author appearances write:
Author Appearances, Starburst Promotions, P.O. Box 4123
Lancaster, Pennsylvania 17604 or call (717) 293-0939.

Credits:
Cover design by Terry Dugan Design.

POLITICAL CORRECTNESS EXPOSED

First Printing, October 1994

ISBN: 0-914984-62-4
Library of Congress Catalog Number 94-66615
Printed in the United States of America.

This book is dedicated to the victims
of
Political Correctness,

the people who will suffer physical and spiritual death
because they believe the lies. If one person comes to know
the truth about the deceit of Political Correctness because of
this book, it will have been a great success.

Contents

Introduction

A little over two years ago I opened a microphone at a local radio station and began hosting a daily phone-in program. Those broadcasts triggered events that led me to the word processor, and the task of writing this book.

I spent nearly six hours a day preparing for my one hour programs, immersing myself in newspapers, magazines, books, TV, and radio. As I prepared for the daily programs, I gradually became depressed. My depression was brought on by a plethora of daily events that depicted the country I so dearly loved as a nation in serious trouble. Each day I reported on episodes of depravity and meanness that slammed into my spirit like alerts that America was literally going to hell.

Things got so bad that my doctor diagnosed my condition as clinical depression. He prescribed a mild medication. The medication helped some, but the gloomy feeling of desperation lingered. It wasn't until I made a total commitment to fight for my country that I began feeling better than I had in years.

Soon after I went on the air, I met two men who greatly influenced me. Pastors Jim Dixon of Resurrection Power Church and Jim Franklin of First Assembly of God made important contributions to my radio programs, and to my new way of thinking. These pastors sponsored lectures by Christian teachers such as Bob DeMoss of the *Focus on the Family* Organization and Jerry Johnson. I interviewed these men on the air, and was I introduced to an exciting and optimistic view of what was happening in America.

These Pastors, and visiting teachers, confirmed everything I had been saying about the dilemma of our nation. They offered sensible pathological accounts of how we have gotten into this mess. Most importantly, they offered workable strategies for solving our Nation's problems. I began to recognize a convergence of conservatism with Christianity.

After a short time of hosting the radio show, I began to introduce myself as a right-wing Conservative, Irish heterosexual, radical-for-Jesus Christian. When I examine the behavior of the religious liberal left (more about this later) I am delighted to be both Conservative and Christian.

Some pastors avoid talking about anything not directly related to the Bible, God's promises and commands, or how to earn salvation by living according to God's Word. These pastors undoubtedly help some of their parishioners, but they fail miserably in attempting to block out or ignore what is happening in the world. One fellow pastor asked me, "How can you call yourself a pastor when you spend so much time talking about politics, movies, TV, education and the world?" My reply was, "How can you call yourself a pastor and not talk about those things?"

Please don't miss the point. While I stress the Word of God, and the urgent need to be armed with His truth, I also teach that it is foolish to go tromping around in hostile territory without knowing the identity of the enemy or comprehending his tactics. Christian communicators, journalists, broadcasters, and teachers have a responsibility to keep Christians informed of the daily deceptions in life.

A few weeks ago I listened to a nationally-broadcasted Christian talk-radio show. The host and his first caller spent twenty-three minutes telling each other about the wonderful time they had experienced at a revival. The message was relevant, but it was repeated over and over as those two men talked about something in which most of their listeners had no interest. I wondered as I listened, "Is this the best these fellows can do with an opportunity to reach millions of listeners?"

My personal opinion about Christian radio, and its enormous potential to educate and inform, was expressed in the cover story of the July 17, 1993 issue of World Magazine. The story reported that many listeners of Christian radio have switched to secular stations to hear people like Rush Limbaugh tell them what is happening in the world. The article reported that First Assembly of God in Charlotte, North Carolina, is holding group meetings to compare Mr. Limbaugh's pronouncements to evangelical teachings.

The Christian who knows God's Word, but is ignorant of the world, may not know that the public school his children attend is influenced by those who want to distribute condoms, secretly advise pregnant children to have abortions, and teach elementary school children about the wonders of homosexuality. The Christian who does not know about such patriotic-sounding organizations as American Civil Liberties Union, National Organization for Women, and People for the American Way, may not know that the very practice of his Christian faith is threatened by these organizations.

Family life can't be lived in a monastery. Christians must, therefore, be able to discern between the truth and Political Correctness. Discernment requires knowledge.

I agree with the conclusions made about Christian radio in World Magazine. Station managers should go after the audience lost to Limbaugh, et.al. Christian listeners deserve dynamic, fast-paced and timely programs that arm them, not only with the truth, but with an understanding of the lies they hear daily.

As my radio programs continued, I became increasingly convinced that a war is being waged for the hearts, minds and souls of America's youth. Decent people everywhere are being shaken awake from a slumber to find that many seemingly impregnable institutions, such as our public schools, and even some of our churches, had been taken over by an enemy that is winning many crucial battles by default.

Often I have longed to get back into military service. For me, it means the front lines. There is probably a warrior gene in my DNA that drives me to rush into the heart of conflicts. I was an Airborne Ranger Infantry Recon Platoon Leader during my first tour in Vietnam, and an advisor to the CIA's Project Phoenix during my second trip. In this current war I had been snipping away at the enemy, with my radio program, but I wanted more. I wanted to be commissioned to join the elite troops in the heart of the fray.

I recognized the enemy's obvious intent to desecrate anything that gave honor to God. It was clear that the heart of this fight was being fought by the men and women of God's army. I decided to join the best fighters I could find, to become a minister. My first challenge was to join the right army. I had been raised as a Roman Catholic, but because I had been divorced, I had been denied the sacraments. There seemed to be no place for me in the Catholic Church.

The Protestant pastors of Las Cruces had presented some of the most positive role models I had ever seen. I was very close to choosing a protestant seminary when I met Bishop Don DeCordova, Catholic Apostolic Bishop of Santa Fe. Within hours of meeting this man I decided to become a Catholic Apostolic Priest.

Our Church combines the liturgy of the Catholic Church prior to Rome's break with Constantinople, with the evangelical spirit being revived in America today. Our Priests marry, as they did for over 1,000 years in the early Catholic Church, we pray directly to God, and we emphasize biblical teachings. My ordination was made more special to me by the fact that I had three Protestant pastors there to pray for my ministry.

I report in these pages the cooperation I have witnessed between many faiths because I perceive the growth of a Christian army as essential to victory in the war. For years, pastors have emphasized the differences in denominations. Our differences are trivial, compared to the fact that we all believe that our God became man, suffered, died, was buried, rose again on the third day so that sins could be forgiven, and He will come again. When the seventy percent plus American Christians come together, we can do things like expose the propaganda of the estimated one percent of the homosexuals in this country to the nonsense it really is. Meanwhile, homosexual unity and commitment threaten many core beliefs of Christianity. Christians simply cannot afford not to lock arms and form impenetrable boundaries around our fundamental right to love, praise and live according to the teachings of Jesus Christ.

Former U.S. Secretary of Education, William Bennett, wrote a pamphlet titled *The Index Of Leading Cultural Indicators*. In his report he revealed that in the past thirty years violent crime has gone up 500 percent, illegitimate births have gone up over 400 percent, divorces have quadrupled, teenage suicide is up 200 percent, and while education costs soared, SAT scores dropped 80 points.

When novelist Walker Percy was asked his greatest fear for America he responded, "Probably the fear of seeing America, with all of its great strength and beauty and freedom . . . gradually subside into decay through default and be defeated, not by the Communist movement, demonstrably a bankrupt system, but from within by weariness, boredom, cynicism, greed and in the end helplessness before its great problems."

Another novelist, John Updike, expressed a similar idea, "The fact that, compared to the inhabitants of Africa and Russia, we still live well, we cannot ease the pain of feeling we no longer live nobly."

The timeliness of mobilizing Christians in America was expressed succinctly by Mother Teresa. While she was visiting America, Mother Teresa was asked, "What do you believe is the poorest of all the countries you have seen?" Without hesitation she replied, "This one."

I agree with Mother Teresa. Despite the fact that our Gross National Product has increased forty-one percent in the past thirty years, we remain a nation of poverty. We can't claim wealth and success as long as the greatest fear of inner-city pre-schoolers is being shot.

I couldn't be happier if this book were mandatory reading only for sinners. Of course we all sin. Christians, however, know that sin calls for immediate correction and resolve to sin no more. The sinners of the '90s seem to revel in their sins. My father used the heathens of our town for instructional purposes, telling me to avoid living as they lived. Today heathenism is chic, an apparent goal of many. As you read over these few verses from II Timothy Chapter 3, think of this week's guest lists for the Phil Donahue and Sally Jesse Raphael shows.

For men shall be lovers of their own selves, covetous, boasters, proud, blasphemers, disobedient to parents, unthankful, unholy, without natural affection, trucebreakers, false accusers, incontinent, fierce, despisers of those that are good, traitors, heady, high-minded, lovers of pleasures more than lovers of God, having a form of godliness, but denying the power thereof: from such turn away. For of this sort are they that which creep into houses, and lead captive silly women laden with sins, led away with divers lusts, ever learning, and never able to come to the knowledge of the truth.

Chapter 1

A Piranha is Only a Fish

DOTs and PCLs

Throughout this book I will refer to a Politically Correct lie, as a PCL (pronounced pickle). I was tempted to save even more space by dropping the "lie" part. The second abbreviation is a communication for the antidote for a PCL, a "dose of truth" or a DOT.

The bad news is that there are so many PCLs that a book is needed to describe them all. The good news is that a DOT exists for every single pickle.

Piranha in Your Bathtub

In the village of Nicety the people were all very happy, exceptionally happy. They were so happy that if one of them was having a horrible day, and you asked how he was doing he would inevitably smile and answer, "Fine, just fine! How are you?"

The residents of Nicety got along all of the time, and the very rare words of discord were always followed immediately by apologies. If there was a single governing rule of life in Nicety it was simply, "Don't annoy anyone."

One night while the nice people of Nicety were sound asleep, an angry-looking man arrived in town. He erected a shack down by the pond where the children played. If the newcomer slept at all that first night he was up and wide awake at the first light.

The man, who called himself Mr. Saton, laughed and told the people that his name had nothing to do with anyone who had a similar name. Because the people of Nicety were so nice they never questioned Mr. Saton about his familiar-sounding name.

Mr. Saton set about the task of amusing the children on the bank of the pond. About half-way through that first morning when Mr. Saton was in Nicety, little Ben Mortis waded out into the pond. The small boy had only gone a few feet from the shore when a great school of fish began to eat him.

"Piranha! Piranha!" shouted little Ben's mother. "The Piranha are eating my baby." Mr. Saton walked over to the screaming woman, and said in a very calm voice, "They're only fish."

Many of the other nice mothers of Nicety witnessed the event. Little Ben had virtually disappeared in a few seconds, so he certainly wasn't annoying anyone. On the other hand, Mrs. Mortis was screaming, and that annoyed them all. Without the slightest hesitation the women all joined Mr. Saton, gathering around Mrs. Mortis and saying in calm voices, "They're only fish."

After a few minutes the calm speaking women shifted from speaking calmly to chanting. The chanting was low in volume, and slow in pentameter, and it seemed as if it could go on forever. The chant was:

> "They're only fish.
> They're only fish.
> They're only fish."

After about twenty minutes of chanting the nice Mrs. Mortis stopped screaming about the Piranha and began to chant, "They're only fish."

Through the rest of that day, and in the many days that followed two-and-a-half children were eaten, and several children lost limbs. Nearly all of the children lost fingers and toes. On some days the children would beg not to go in the water, but their parents, along with Mr. Saton, told them, "They're only fish," and forced them into the water.

One day a man from a major TV network came to investigate stories of Piranha in the pond. On the national news that evening he ended his investigative report by saying, "There have been some complaints, but they can't be taken seriously, because after all, they're only fish."

One day a man far from Nicety went on the radio and told millions of listeners that the people of Nicety were allowing their children to be eaten by Piranha. The people of Nicety were very annoyed by the man on the radio. They began putting the Piranha into their bathtubs to demonstrate that they were only fish.

Soon the man on the radio was being called a troublemaker, a radical and a fanatic. The people who ridiculed the man on the radio were upset because the Piranha in the Nicety Pond were, after all, only fish.

This Will Kill Ya!

My wife proofed the first draft of this book, and was appalled by the story of the little children being eaten by Piranha. She argued that nothing justified adding to the violence in America. Because she is so often right, I gave it a lot of thought. The story is of course an analogy of how PCLs grow. I finally decided to leave the violent part of the story in this text because you can't approach an understanding of PCLs until you realize that our children are dying daily because of the lies they are being told.

Children who are being told that safe sex means using condoms when they have intercourse might believe that PCL. I interviewed a 12-year-old girl on my radio program. I asked the girl what she was being told in a Middle School about sex. She said, "They teach us that we gotta have safe sex." The optimum words here are, " **. . . We Gotta Have . . . Sex . . .**" Certainly some of these children who accept the "safe sex" PCL will contract AIDS and die. These deaths will be directly attributable to the PCLs. PCLs kill people.

Hey World! How About My Shorts?

Here is an example of how a PCL is merchandized, and how it influences society:

A few years ago Michael Jackson had a debut of a new video on national television. In the video he did something every male's parents have taught him to never do in public. Michael grabbed his shorts, as if the gesture had some special communication for his fans. I suppose the meaning intended was something like, "Hey look here, folks. I'm a boy child. Isn't that something?" I personally believe a more accurate interpretation of the meaning of the gesture is, "Hey, Gang, look where my brain has migrated!"

Mr. Jackson, because of his enormous popularity, gave credibility to the gesture as a means of communication. Crotch-grabbing has become a sort of trademark for Michael Jackson. Imagine this, America; here is a man who communicates to his fans with a gesture most of your mothers would never tolerate in her home.

So, we have a grown man with a disgusting habit. Perhaps there is a homeless person who hangs around the post office in your home town who has the same habit. Here is the difference. Michael Jackson made huge money deals to promote Pepsi and Sony. (I then started drinking Coke.) Michael Jackson performed at half-time during the Super Bowl. Michael Jackson has become a sort of patron-saint of Liz Taylor. Michael Jackson, and his behavior, which includes the tributes he continuously pays to his shorts, have become institutions.

Mr. Jackson is so *Politically Correct* that we have become comfortable with his crotch-grabbing. The psychologists explain a phenomena called *systematic desensitization*. A person can be exposed to a stimulus so many times that the stimulus ceases to stimulate. We have seen Michael Jackson grab his shorts so many times we barely realize what we are seeing. When simultaneous stories broke concerning allegations of child abuse and cancellations of performances of Mr. Jackson's Tour, U.S. TV newscasts were packed with footage of Mr. Jackson, wearing a golden diaper over leotards, on stage, grabbing his shorts. Michael Jackson even began wearing a head-mounted microphone so he could conduct spot-checks on his manhood with either or both hands.

The fact that we have sunk to a level of unconsciousness that prohibits us from responding to the crudity of crotch-grabbing may not seem significant to some. Last week I observed an incident in front of our local high school. A male and female student were communicating with hand gestures across a busy street. They were giving each other the Michael Jackson salute while a hundred or so students laughed and cheered. I am appalled that Michael Jackson, Pepsi, Sony, The Super Bowl Planning Committee, Liz Taylor, MTV, and major networks have all contributed to the institutionalizing of the PCL that crotch-grabbing is chic.

The underwear salute has not gone unnoticed by those who want the same level of fame as Mr. Jackson. The new breed of country music artists are trading talent for vulgarity. Larry Gatlin reportedly said that he was probably over the hill because he wouldn't grab his crotch on stage. Keep in mind that with forums like the Grand Ole Opry and Branson, Missouri, the core of country music fans has been families for decades. It will be interesting to see if the country music industry attempts to drag their fans down to the MTV level of behavior, or maintain a modicum of human decency.

Political Correctness is a movement that often endorses the crudest and host humanly demeaning of behaviors, and institutionalizes those behaviors through systematic desensitization of the public.

Fuddy Duddy Rides Again

Inevitably, many will respond to my writing about Michael Jackson with a resounding, "So What?" It's probably true that not a single person will experience brain damage, heart failure, or even a sprained wrist from crotch-grabbing. The next question should be, "What's the big deal?"

The "big deal" is that people do have responsibility for their behavior. The "big deal" is that many adolescents are so impressionable that any role model, positive or negative, has the ability to shape behavior.

Consider the teenage girls in San Antonio who passed an initiation into a gang by having sex with a known AIDS victim. They had to understand that the very real risk of a slow and miserable death was probable, but their intense desire to be accepted by a gang of fellow misfits overrode common sense.

One teenager in a State detention facility told me that he had agreed to perform oral sex on other boys for a cigarette. Then he told me that he knew the other boys were lying about the cigarettes. He also told me he found homosexual acts abhorrent. "Then why did you do it?" I asked. He answered, "Because I at least got their attention."

In a college psychology course I watched a film titled *The Lottery*. The plot concerned a village where a monthly lottery occurred. Each citizen was given a number and the person with *the* number, was executed. The film illustrated the sheer power of socially-accepted ritual and belief. Probably no subculture in our country is more susceptible to accepted rituals than children.

American children, with a diminishing sense of family and family rituals, are driven to develop a behavioral pattern that leads to a sense of self, an identity. Considering the fact that an average American six-year-old boy has spent more time watching TV than he will spend with his father during his entire lifetime, the minds of children are like open buckets waiting to be filled. This is not a condemnation of children. There are many children who have been guided in learning discernment. My point is that many children are unwitting victims of TV and movie producers, entertainers, athletes, etc.

Jesus Christ was about as specific as He ever was when He described the fate of people who lead children astray. In Matthew 18: 6. He said, *But who so shall offend one of these little ones who believes in me, it were better for him that a millstone were hanged around his neck, and that he were drown in the depth of the sea.* Any questions?

Beliefs = Values = Behavior

One of the most reliable benchmarks of noble living in a civilization is the respect people acknowledge for behavioral boundaries. There were ancient civilizations that routinely killed slaves for sport and sacrificed babies to their gods. Those behaviors cross our moral boundaries, and could not be accepted in the U.S. Not by all! Not yet!

One means of evaluating progress is to examine societal acceptance of changes in boundaries. For example, I attended high school in Birmingham, Alabama in the late 1950s. (There were about a dozen high schools in and around Birmingham.) I remember seeing a pregnant girl in summer school, and the memory of that expectant mother walking down the steps of Phillip's High School stuck in my mind as a rare thing to see. Compare that environment to a small school in New Mexico. The principal told me that his number one problem was teen pregnancy.

Teen pregnancy is the direct result of a PCL. The PCL is a belief that "Kids are going to do it (have sex) anyway." The belief includes submission on the parts of parents and teachers trying to raise their children chaste. "They are going to do it anyway," presupposes that chastity is an impossibility.

Acceptance of "Chastity is impossible and promiscuity is inevitable" is a cockeyed belief system. That belief system demands an equally cockeyed set of values, such as, "Its okay for my kids to have sex in my home," or "They'll grow out of this stage, so I'll just make sure they have condoms."

With cockeyed beliefs and values in place, the disintegration of behavior is a "given." As all boundaries of human decency are dissolved the behavior becomes increasingly debase. Weeks before I began this writing I heard a news report of a twelve-year-old boy who was abused at a birthday party given by his parents. The parents paid a stripper to entertain, and watched with delight as their son had sexual contact with the woman. This could only make sense to people who believed, "They're going to do it anyway," and had congruent values.

I tell my parishioners not to conduct social conversations in our chapel. The chapel is a room exclusively designed for conversation with God, and the conducting of worldly business shows lack of respect for the presence of God in that room. Granted, those conversations are relatively insignificant. The conversations are, however, a crossing of boundaries that should be maintained in a chapel.

Boundaries come in systems, or package deals. When boundaries are accepted there are no *little* things. Consistency in behavior means always respecting boundaries, even the so-called little ones.

Coach Bear Bryant set many records for winning while coaching at the University of Alabama. He told his football players, "As long as you are on this football field, do everything 100 percent. If you bend over to tie your shoes, do that 100 percent." Coach Bryant's obvious belief was, "Everything is important." This belief led to a value of, "We practice over and over until we do everything as well as it can be done." The resulting behavior was development of a football dynasty at the University of Alabama.

Coach Bryant didn't believe in going 100 percent on the field and half-way in other areas. He was a 100 percent leader. When his star quarterback, Joe Namath, broke Coach Bryant's training rules, the Coach suspended his star. Joe violated one of Coach Braynt's boundaries, and he had to accept the consequences.

Coach Bryant's philosophy about the importance of little things, is crotch-grabbing doesn't make people pregnant. Crotch-grabbing is an erosion of the boundary of sexual self-respect. I am convinced that crotch-grabbing in public and the rise of teen pregnancies are as surely related as tying your football shoes and touchdowns are related.

A survey repeated in two states was administered to middle school children. In both states, close to a third of those children believed that a male having sex with a resisting female did not constitute rape. A high school group calling themselves the Spur's Posse, kept score of how many girls they had *scored* with sexually. Some of the boys' parents jokingly encouraged them, even though some of the female victims were resisting 12-year-olds.

Crotch-grabbing is not rape, but the activities are related. A well-behaved adolescent who sets a boundary and won't grab his crotch as a substitute for waving, probably won't rape small girls and call it sport. A teenager who can discern that even someone with the celebrity status of Michael Jackson can be dead wrong, will very likely also know that rape is wrong.

Talking Wrong

Comedian Steve Martin did a routine in which he asked his audience in a conspiratorial tone, "Want to have some fun?" Mr. Martin then suggested that it was great fun to "talk wrong" to children. The comedian then demonstrated talking nonsense, putting words together in a great confusion of meaningless talk.

There is a lot of "Wrong Talking" being done in our country, and its not just a silly prank. After hearing on a national broadcast about the plight of Mr. Jim Moore in Houston, Texas I gave him a phone call. Mr. Moore was an AIDS victim, and as I talked to him it became obvious that he was in the final days of his life. We set up an interview, and that very sick man told my listeners his story.

Jim Moore had been a teacher and a coach at a High School in the Houston area. Jim was an athlete himself and ran over five miles a day with the teenagers he coached. Jim had been involved in what he described only as high-risk sexual activity. As a teacher and coach he had been cautioning his students to use condoms during sexual activity. He had been a victim of the safe sex PCL, and believing that a condom protected him.

When Jim Moore was in the final stages of his disease he went, in a withered condition, to speak before an assembly in the school where he had taught. Mr. Moore's mere presence was an ominous reminder that he had been a victim of "wrong talking."

The PCL Merchants

Dr. Ruth Westheimer and Madonna teamed up to perform at an AIDS benefit. Madonna walked around topless, displaying the talent to undress most one-year-old babies have mastered. Dr. Ruth managed to wiggle into a black rubber nurse's uniform. You might have trouble understanding what this duo's behavior had to do with prevention or cure for AIDS, but that doesn't matter. Dr. Ruth and Madonna were so Politically Correct that their audience loved them.

In the same week of the AIDS benefit Dr. Ruth appeared on the Phil Donahue program, rubber nurse uniform and all. Donahue introduced her as someone who has always been "Politically Correct." Really! He actually said that! Dr. Ruth then suggested that young people who want to have sex should use brightly colored condoms, perhaps even glow in the dark models, to make their experience more enjoyable.

There, on national television, was a geriatric, giggling psychiatrist, giving out some of the worst advise imaginable. (This is not my subjective opinion, but it is documented fact (see Chapter seven). Sitting beside the Doctor, was Phil Donahue, one of the most renowned broadcasters in America, agreeing with Dr. Ruth's every word, and reminding his listeners that the Doctor had always been Politically Correct.

Donahue didn't crack a smile when he talked about Political Correctness. It was as if he had unraveled an ancient scroll and read directly from the word of God that Dr. Ruth and everything she said was right and true. I believe that Donahue does indeed feel that the ultimate certificate of authentication and proof positive of truth, is Political Correctness.

When I first heard the term Political Correctness I thought it was a joke about some "hair-brained" professor who believed his opinions were infallible truths. I thought that, at the very least, Political Correctness was a creation of Conservatives to illustrate how arrogant and self-righteous Liberals could be. It's no joke. The same week Dr. Ruth received the P.C. stamp of approval from Donahue, I heard a straight-faced Bryant Gumble talk with devotion about a man who was "Politically Correct." To people like Donahue and Bryant Gumble, Political Correctness is a sort of Mazeltov from God.

Political Correctness is on its way to becoming the group think of the '90s. One of the reasons for its power and growth is the perceived status of the people who originate many of the PCLs.

A patient at a large psychiatric hospital constantly told the staff about how the sun was sending out a laser light and burning a hole in his forehead. All of the staff dutifully recorded his comments on his chart, but not one of them ever called the national weather bureau, the FBI or their congressperson to alert them about the rays coming from the sun. The psychiatric patient lacked the status to change the way people felt and thought. One can only wonder what would happen if the story about the sun's evil rays were released by Tom Brokaw or Mike Wallace.

Television personalities have tremendous power to influence human thought. An anchorman, for example, can discredit a guest with something as subtle as a chuckle or an upturned eyebrow. On the other hand, an anchorman can contribute enormous credibility to a guest by the way he phrases questions. During the '92 presidential election, Bryant Gumble interviewed candidate Clinton. He visibly gushed over the man, as he discussed Mr. Clinton's bus tour. He asked for a description of what it must feel like to have all of those people looking at Mr. Clinton and listening to him with such hope and appreciation. Bryant Gumble made a campaign bus tour sound at least as significant as the Sermon on The Mount, and he appeared to be putting Mr. Clinton in the same category as the speaker at the Sermon on The Mount.

There are still millions of people who believe that if they see something on TV it must be true. Have you ever seen merchandise in a store with a sticker that read, "As Advertised On TV." Those stickers wouldn't be used if millions of people didn't believe that television represents truth. TV personalities are fully aware of the power they command, and they use that power like the communications experts they are.

In the early 1970s British Broadcasting Corporation (BBC) made major changes in the way they presented the news. They fired all of those elegant-sounding people who put such energy and passion into their deliveries. BBC replaced those people with a more subdued crop of people they called news readers.

called news readers. They attempted to report the news in such a deadpan fashion as to conceal any hint of personal opinion on the events being reported. The closest American television comes to objective reporting is C-SPAN. I have watched some of their reporters for months without knowing their political ideology. Compare that objectivity to the major networks where much news favorable to conservatism, or damning to liberalism is simply not reported.

The average child watches television about six hours a day. Meanwhile, there are millions of Americans who snatch ten or fifteen minutes of the *Today* show or *Nightline* once a week. Those people form many of their opinions based on the word bytes of the people holding the microphones. Busy people don't have the time to unravel the PCLs they hear and get to the truth. Television is a forum that makes the messengers capable of doing massive shape changes with the messages.

It is a politically *incorrect* belief that:

If enough people who look like network anchor-persons say anything eloquently, often enough, a lot of people will begin to believe what is being said.

PCL Merchants With Much Bigger Screens

There is a Mecca for radical left-wing causes. Its called *Hollywood*. At any given Academy Awards Ceremony you will hear at least as many speeches for left-wing causes as you will hear at a National Democratic Convention.

I can count the "out of the closet" conservatives in Hollywood, and not come close to ten. Meanwhile, Jane Fonda, who cornered the market on far-left politics in the '60s, appears sedate and calm compared to the current crop of "Hollywoodies."

The power to influence is not overlooked by some of the more militant directors such as Rob Rheiner. These people openly talk about "The Cause." Rheiner appears in a cameo role in *Sleepless In Seattle*, long enough to get in a plug about condom usage. These crusaders-with-cameras, embed liberal messages in their movies with all the subtlety of stampeding elephants.

Movie Critic, Michael Medved reported that Hollywood lost money for a decade, while making movies that families avoided. It seemed as though Hollywood was on a campaign to lower the standards of language, sexual behavior and human decency in America. They persisted in producing filth that fewer and fewer people were willing to consume, even when it was obvious that wholesome entertainment equated to big money.

The Disney Movie *The Rocketeer*, was a kid's adventure flick, released in the summer. It was almost, not quite, but almost the kind of movie my Dad used to take me to see. The movie included a scene of a man enunciating the words for S.O.B. Walt Disney would never have allowed that shoddy example of movie-making to be released under his name. Walt Disney encouraged J. Edgar Hoover to screen his movies, so that nothing he produced would ever harm our country or its citizens. The director of *The Rocketeer* must have had one of two intentions. Situation one is that he just wanted to make a movie, and he really didn't know that many families don't tolerate that kind of language in their homes, and wouldn't want their children to hear it. Situation two is that he had a mission to teach people that dropping standards of language was acceptable. I must believe the truth is that the producer was campaigning for filth because, with regard to the ignorance theory, no one could really be that stupid. Could they?

I doubt the sincerity of many of the "Hollywoodies." The sheer improbability of that many people, in one place, being that liberal, defies all that is known about statistics. Liberalism is so Politically Correct in Tinsel Town that choosing some left-wing cause appears to be a wise career move. Some of the more popular causes now are radical militant environmentalism, feminism, homosexuality, cross-dressing, and anything that smacks of an anti-God theme.

I won't end this chapter without acknowledging what might be the signs of a new trend in Hollywood. In recent month's movies such as *Free Willie* and *Lorenzo's Oil* have reminded a lot of people of the wonderful work Hollywood can produce. I hope the trend grows and continues, so I can stop communicating so derisively about an industry capable of such great work.

Chapter 2

The Religous Left

Spotting PCLs

Humans require oxygen and water. Cannonballs sink in water. Winter in Siberia is colder than Summer in Phoenix, and eagles fly while fish swim. Not one of these statements has ever received the endorsement of Political Correctness. They don't need to be PCLs because they all are irrefutably true. True statements don't need the artificial reinforcement of Political Correctness.

Politically Correct statements are almost always lies. Without the support of Political Correctness a PCL lacks the strength required for survival. While most PCLs are lies, all lies are not PCLs. Some are designed to attack the truth which offends only a few radicals. Examples of lies that never qualify for PCL status are, "Smoking Doesn't cause Cancer," "There was no holocaust," and "The world ends Saturday at noon." These lies don't benefit enough people to merit PCL status.

PCLs benefit people. In the mid 1980s a TV Commercial ran for several months on national television. The commercial featured a beautiful woman looking into the camera and talking. Her dialogue went something like this, "Hello. I'm Olga Fisbo (Not her real name.) I'm a movie star, and my appearance is important. That's why I use 'Brand X' for my skin." I thought, "What a gorgeous lady! Why haven't I seen any of her movies? I'll bet she is a wonderful actress." About six months later I saw a comedy skit with people asking, "Who in the heck is Olga Fisbo?"

I never met anyone who had seen Olga Fisbo in a movie. If she actually was a "Movie Star" she had been an obscure one. Reality didn't matter, however, because a lot of people just accepted the notion that Olga was a "Star." The commercial producers had made Olga's stardom Politically Correct. The purpose was to sell face cream, and I suppose it worked. Most PCLs are sold as subtly as the Olga Fisbo PCL, and they always benefit someone. In searching out the authors of PCLs it is wise to ask, "Who benefits from this?"

Anatomy Of a PCL

The PCL Is

"Kids are going to do it (have sex) anyhow." Take a quick look at who benefits from this PCL.

- Parents who are too lazy or unable to teach their children sexual restraint.
- School Administrators and teachers with a hedonistic agenda.
- Children who want to be relieved of sexual responsibility.
- Pornographers, like Madonna who hawked her book *Sex* as if it were a liberating educational manual.
- Planned Parenthood as it sells abortions.
- The movie and TV industry as they sell programs with sexual adolescent themes (Such as an episode of Doogie Howser, featuring Doogie skinny dipping with an older woman.)
- People Like Donahue and Sally Jesse who can produce programs about perverts, such as parents who allow their children to have sex in their homes.
- Condom companies.
- People philosophically dedicated to the destruction of family values.

- The ACLU, militant feminists, homosexuals, and other groups with strong anti-God, anti-religion, and anti-family agendas.

At least half of the groups named are beneficiaries of the "kids will do it anyway" PCL, and have a primary motivation of making money. Our children are, quite literally, being sold for profit.

The DOT

The Dose of truth that blows the "Kids will do it anyway" PCL literally to hell where it belongs is, *"Abstinence works every single time it's used, and kids can learn it."*

Abstinence programs such as the "Sex Respect" program have been tested in schools, and they reduce teen pregnancies, and stem the spread of Sexually Transmitted Diseases (STDs). Meanwhile, more Politically Correct programs that stress condom distribution have been proven repeatedly to exacerbate every problem they were designed to solve. The documentation is conclusive, yet it is repeatedly ignored. The facts are ignored, because they happen to be Politically Incorrect. A PCL has almost mystical powers of persuasion for Liberals.

An abstinence program with an impressive track record of positive results was introduced into a Shreveport, Louisiana School. Almost immediately the program was challenged in court by the American Civil Liberties Union. In the curriculum it was taught that animals, like human beings, have sex, but that human beings exist on a level higher than animals. The ACLU's complaint was that teaching that humans were on a higher level than animals made the course religious, and was therefore unlawful. This sounds crazy at first, but consider the implications to the PCL. If children were taught that they functioned at levels higher than snail darters and skunks then how could they accept the "Kids are going to do it anyway" PCL? The answer is obvious. If children accepted the fact that maybe they were on a higher level of existence than animals, it would follow that humans could *control* their animal instincts.

It seems to anyone with a walnut sized brain (horse sense) that a program that worked would be preferable to one that didn't. The ACLU ignored the facts and went to court to uphold their PCL. For the ACLU, the PCL had taken on a sort of sacramental or divine status. To fully appreciate how dedicated Liberals can be to causes and programs, it is important to understand the new religious left.

If it Walks Like a Duck, if it Talks Like a Duck . . .

At the 1992 Republican National Convention, Pat Buchanan said that America was in a religious war. The reaction of the liberal media was so immediate and so eruptive that observers recognized a dead giveaway that a core nerve had been struck. Mr. Buchanan succinctly described himself as having been demonized. Mr. Buchanan did more than threaten the left with the one thing they equate to annihilation, the mobilization of the religious right. Mr. Buchanan had come close to exposing the existence of the "fanatical religious left."

Republicans ducked beneath Mr. Buchanan's pronouncement, and modified his words, calling the conflict a cultural war. Pat was right the first time. The war is raging now, and the battle area is defined along religious lines.

People who want to make me politically powerless, and bestow the indelible mark of a buffoon on me accuse me of being on the nefarious "religious right." The implication is that the religious right is a resting place for people so fanatic that anything they say should be immediately discounted as nonsense. Christianity is a religion based on love. There is nothing fanatical about Christianity. Critics will point out the early Christians who chose martyrdom over rejecting their God, calling those martyrs fanatics. The real fanatics were the Romans who offered the Christians those options.

As a Christian, I have the extreme good fortune of not being answerable to anyone but a just and loving Father, my God. Mocking from other men is a mere fulfillment of prophecy such as in Jude 18, *How that they told you there should be mockers in the last time, who should walk after their own ungodly lusts.*

It is fanaticism that people fear. Liberals love to cite examples of so-called Christians gone "whacko," and characterize the craziest as typical of all Christians. These same people who try to epitomize Christians with people like Jim Jones usually neglect mention of church sponsored homeless shelters, hospitals, orphanages, halfway houses, soup kitchens, etc. People like Jim Jones did horrible things, but by the objective measurement of lives lost, their acts pale in comparison to the people killed in the world, during the twentieth century, for "political" causes. No one knows, for example, how many people were killed by Joe Stalin. I would suggest that anyone wanting a real appreciation of fanaticism run-amuck, visit the Holocaust Museum in Washington, D.C.

I welcome being identified with the religious right. As a Catholic Apostolic Priest, I hope the day never comes when I feel even a small drop of shame at being called religious. As for being on the right, I am again comforted by an examination of the ranks of the left. Being called religious and right is, for me, both accurate and complimentary. My dictionary definition of religious includes, " . . . belief upheld with zeal and devotion." When carried to the extreme of fanaticism, the zeal and devotion is much more apparent among Liberals than it is among conservative citizens who proclaim that they are religious.

Consider the "zeal and devotion," of President Clinton's Surgeon General, Dr. Joycelyn Elders. For years Dr. Elders has been a devout distributor of condoms to school children. In the Arkansas counties where her condom-distribution schemes were implemented, both the teen pregnancy and the STD rates rose dramatically. Clearly, her method did not then, and still does not work. With her "zeal and devotion" to the "Kids are going to do it anyway" PCL, Dr. Elders clings to a plan doomed to fail.

In Arkansas, Dr. Elders distributed thousands of defective condoms. The defective condoms distributed by Dr. Elders were ten times less reliable than the condoms she had distributed earlier. So she went around to the clinics where the condoms had been distributed, and exchanged the faulty ones for new condoms that still were subject to appalling failure rates.

This was the work of a medical doctor, who had taken an oath to do no harm. Can you imagine more serious harm being done to people who believe condoms will protect them from AIDS than distributing faulty condoms, and then saying nothing? Dr. Elders refused to make a public announcement or a recall of the faulty condoms already distributed. That amounted to an attempt at genocide, and had to have had life and death consequences, especially among homosexuals. I still am puzzled that groups like "Act Up" didn't go ballistic when the story broke of Dr. Elders' deception.

When asked why she didn't make any public announcements, Dr. Elders answered, "I didn't want to hurt the program." The "Program" is condom distribution, and only one thing could explain Dr. Elders' silence. The only plausible explanation is that the Liberals have elevated condom distribution to the sacramental level. Homosexuals would only sit still for very real genocide if they valued the Political Correctness of condom distribution over their very lives. Dr. Elders would not be so ignorant as to cover up such a scandalous event unless she had elevated the "Program" to a status that superceded common sense and human decency. I call that "zeal and devotion."

Don't Look Down

There is wisdom in telling someone who is dangling from a cliff, "Don't look down." If the person looks down he will be confronted with the severity of his dilemma. Some Liberals never "look down," and use tremendous energy ignoring reality.

Consider the mental and spiritual gymnastics Liberals have to go through to keep reality opposed beliefs alive. The pro-abortion people call themselves "pro-choice," yet they ignore 1.6 million babies a year who have no choice at all. They talk about a woman's right to control her body, yet over half of those killed are female. They are cautious to avoid calling an unborn baby anything but a viable tissue mass. Staffers in abortion clinics are instructed to avoid letting mothers see ultra sound pictures of their babies. Those photos look more like babies than they look like viable tissue mass. If the baby is truly a "tissue mass," what could be wrong with letting the mother see a photo? Certainly a mother wouldn't begin any sort of bonding process with viable tissue mass just because "it" looked like a baby. If Christians were as diligent at avoiding sin as abortionists were at tap-dancing around the facts, the angels would sing for days. It takes nothing short of religious zeal and devotion to numb out what goes on in abortion clinics.

What I Say, Not What I Do

A very telling sign of religious fanaticism on the left is their deep belief that they are the chosen people, a special group singled out for great privilege. Consider the elitist attitude of a liberal congress that passed a restrictive family leave bill, and immediately exempted themselves from their own mischief.

Remember how many Clinton appointees had neglected to pay into the social security funds of their servants? One lawyer tried to wiggle out of those charges by saying he and his maid were lifelong friends. I suppose that fellow invites all of his pals and buddies over to scrub out his toilets and mop his floors.

Liberals believe laws, rules and regulations are things that other people should follow. They of course, don't need to bother with such trivial matters, because they are the chosen people.

Liberals pride themselves on being tolerant, and their willingness to encourage diversity. Their tolerance ends abruptly when the diversity becomes *politically incorrect*. Liberals are totally intolerant of Christianity, anything vaguely related to traditional family values, or patriotism.

One day a caller to my radio program demonstrated the industrial strength version of the liberal elitist thought process. She began with the old liberal knee jerk opening, calling me a lot of names my Mom never allowed in her home, because I was so rude. (I can't count the times I have been taken to task by Liberals for rudeness, while they said things about me that I would never say about anyone. They really don't realize they are doing that.) As a joke I asked the caller, "Do you actually believe that everything you say is absolutely correct, and that you have some special access to the truth?" In less than a second she answered, "Yes!" It was no joke to her. She was protected by the armor of Political Correctness, and therefore had a monopoly on infallible truth. This was a true believer.

Liberals know their doctrine. They aren't burdened with the need to check Scriptures because their priests, like Donahue and Sally Jesse, teach daily the high tenets of Political Correctness. The religious warfare is in full swing, and no wonder the left didn't want Conservatives to know it was happening. The left is alive, well and fully mobilized. Our side, meanwhile, keeps talking about a wake up call. If the right doesn't wake up soon we could lose the great religious war of the '90s by default.

The New Age Connection

Political Correctness is supportive of that which benefits Political Correctness. The New Age Religions are very complimentary to Political Correctness. The core beliefs of the New Age Religions are that each person is a deity unto himself. This belief opens the door for the personal fashioning of morality, and for the abandonment of beliefs so burdensome as moral absolutes. With fundamental restrictions such as the ten commandments out of the way, the New Agers are free to consider such moral issues as, "Is this modern, chic, and in keeping with Political Correctness?" In many ways New Age Religion is the religion of Political Correctness.

With the Liberals manifesting their own religion of Political Correctness, and sympathetic to the New Age Religions, they are free to focus on their arch enemy, Fundamentalist Religion. Many think of Fundamentalist Religion as Full Gospel Christians, leaning toward legalism. Certainly, a gathering of ministers from Protestant and Catholic churches would probably all differ in their beliefs of which churches were really fundamentalist. This book is not focused on the divergence of Christian perspectives, but on the beliefs and behaviors of the Politically Correct. The more liberal of the Politically Correct believe that Fundamentalism encompasses any who attempt to adhere to a code of conduct based on God's instructions regarding "right and wrong behavior." Nothing is more directly contradictory to the core (if it feels good do it) beliefs of Political Correctness than Christianity. Political Correctness abhors law and rule, and calls those things restrictions. Christianity embraces law and welcomes the gift of discernment.

Christian Bashing

For a group of people who profess tolerance as their superlative virtue, the Politically Correct abandon all tolerance for Christianity and attack it with a vengeance. The April 1993 issue of the School Board Journal pictured five people seated at a table beneath the shadow of a sinister, looming eagle. The caption read, "Is your school board under the shadow of the radical right-wing." Christian bashing has become a very popular, and a very profitable activity.

At an educators workshop in Denver, Colorado, in May, 1993, two-hundred plus educators paid registration fees of

$397 (Taxpayer's money) to attend a workshop titled, "Responding Democratically to Religious Agendas, Right-Wing Pressure Groups and School Reforms." One speaker was Mr. Frosty Troy, the editor of a liberal, alternative newspaper, The Oklahoma Observer. Mr. Troy's presentation was titled God Squad vs. Public Education. He compared Dr. James Dobson, of Focus on the Family, to Adolph Hitler, and claimed that Dr. Dobson had called President Clinton the Anti-Christ. Dr. Dobson responded by publicly offering Mr. Troy $10,000 to produce a copy of the newsletter with the "Anti-Christ" statements. As usual, there was no response from the Left. Liberals often make accusations that aren't based on fact.

There is often nothing subtle about liberal attacks on Christianity. Theologian Hans Kung has written about a "Death of God" theology. He also reported on the "militant-aggressive atheism" that was essential to the rise of Soviet Socialism. Militant-aggressive atheism is being employed all over America today. Naomi Goldenberg is the author of *The Changing of the Gods: Feminism and the End of Traditional Religions*. Ms. Goldenberg wrote,

"We women are going to bring an end to God. As we take positions in government, in medicine, in business, in the arts, and finally, in religion, we will be the end of Him. . . . The feminist movement in Western Culture is engaged in the slow execution of God and Yahweh."

For decades the guardian of free speech in America was the American Civil Liberties Union. Anything, no matter how outrageous, how hateful, or how inflammatory, could find defense from the ACLU. As late as five years ago, I had a conversation with a social science professor who said, "As radical as some of their causes have been, the ACLU has always been consistent in defending freedom of speech." I agreed then, but I certainly don't now.

During the Spring of 1993, a major dispute broke out in the leadership ranks of the ACLU. The founders of the organization accused the new leadership of ditching "Free Speech Protection" for the more vogue cause of Political Correctness. In fact, the ACLU no longer protects all free speech, but only the free speech of anyone who is not speaking out for Jesus Christ or engaged in the ever-dreaded "P" word, prayer. The ACLU is poised to attack anyone who comes close to enunciating the "P" word.

In the Summer of 1993 the University of South Carolina offered a doctoral seminar titled, "Christian Fundamentalism And Public Education." The course description said, "assist school practitioners and others in understanding the fundamentalist phenomenon and combatting its challenge to public education in a secular democracy." The course instructor, openly homosexual Dr. James T. Sears, author of *Growing Up Gay In The South* said, "If some fundamentalists had their way, the class would be reduced to the reading of the Bible." Dr. Sears, of course, enjoys the protection of Political Correctness.

Ideas blessed by the power of Political Correctness enjoy immunity from attack by the liberal media. Meanwhile, anything oppositional to Political Correctness, specifically Religion, is mean-spirited, intolerant, red-neck bigotry. Name-calling is the silliness of children, but in a world where Political Correctness determines value, name-calling done by the Politically Correct is unfortunately very effective.

Those Ears of Dan

I had a friend in college, and his real name wasn't really Dan. If I wanted to describe Dan so that you could pick him out in a crowd I would tell you to look for a big, usually smiling, kid with big shoulders and humongous ears.

Dan had a funny way of getting to know strangers. He would simply approach people he wanted to know and begin to talk about their enormous ears. Most people never got a chance to insult Dan about his ears. He avoided being insulted by always taking the offensive.

The Politically Correct use a tactic very similar to Dan's "What big ears you have!" maneuver. They are constantly on the warpath against Conservatives and Christians, and most of their attacks are "Cover Ups" for the numerous holes in their philosophy.

Consider the stimulus that sparks the most bombastic liberal attacks, and you usually will uncover a closet they do not want opened. The "Family Values" suggestions in recent years have ignited the most vicious reactions from Liberals. The attacks aren't nearly as much a hatred of family values as they are a cover up of the serendipity arrangements of group gropers, same sex "marriages," etc. they want legitimized.

Liberals cover up the fact of their "big ears" by attacking Conservative Christians. The problem is that the attacks are so vicious and so frequent, that many victims of the attacks begin to actually believe their attackers. Even my friend Dan, on rare occasions, found victims so self-conscious that they became ashamed of their own ears. Dan would always back off at the first sign of condescendence, and apologize. Liberals are not as good-hearted as Dan. If Liberals sense Conservative Christians caving in under their attacks, they go for the kill. The remedy, obviously, is to focus on the truth, and recognize big eared attackers as the tactical straw dogs they really are.

Chapter 3

Mamas Don't Let Your Babies Grow Up to Be Liberals

Efforts to "demonize" Liberals only hurt Conservatives. While their behavior is often deplorable, many Liberals are good people, with the very best of intentions. The problem is that Liberalism not only doesn't work, but tends to cause horrible messes.

Winston Churchill once said that he believed everyone should have enough of the passion of youth to be a Liberal, and live long enough to gain the maturity required to become a Conservative. In this Chapter I'll tell you why Liberalism is so attractive to people who don't think very deeply about things, and why Conservatism almost always provides more enduring solutions to problems.

I was once a Liberal. I voted for McGovern. I am convinced, however, that I am not merely an example of Churchill's theory of Liberals maturing into Conservatives. The Liberalism of the '60s, the J.F.K., and the Hubert Humphrey-type Liberalism has almost nothing to do with the near socialist Clinton brand of Liberalism of the '90s.

The quantum leaps of Liberalism to the left was demonstrated on Rush Limbaugh's Radio Program. Rush played excerpts from speeches of J.F.K. and Hubert Humphrey. These speeches would have been cheered at the 1992 Republican

National Convention. It's also very likely that these same speeches, with trigger phrases like "family values" would have been booed at the Democratic National Convention.

I have no set-in-cement, affiliation with any Political Party. I vote for human beings who have demonstrated a dedication to duty, a willingness to serve, an integrity of word, and an ability to make moral and intelligent decisions. I have voted Democratic in the past, and could do that again. As I write these pages, however, the Democratic National Party is the home of radical Liberalism in America.

Liberalism is no more inherently evil than is Conservatism. It is the extremes of both Liberalism and Conservatism that can demolish the core beliefs of a Democracy. Mainstream Conservatism is so tame today that it is nearly indistinguishable from the American Liberalism of the 1960s. It should be noted that after listening to one of J.F.K's speeches, a Rush Limbaugh fan called Rush and suggested that J.F.K. be named a Ditto-Head (A big fan of Rush's) posthumously. The "Firebrands" or the "Radical Right" of Conservatism today are merely Christians who happen to believe the Ten Commandments make a lot of sense. It is the Clinton Liberals who produced a cabinet that looks like holdovers from Woodstock. While this book is not about Liberalism through the ages, in the next few pages, as I describe Liberalism, I am addressing the Radical, Clinton Liberals of the 1990s in America.

Teacups vs. Bulldozers

How would you fight a forest fire? The Liberal might take a teacup of water, rush up as close to the fire as possible, and douse the fire. Liberals believe that there are quick fixes to everything.

Liberals want to help the poor by passing out money. They want to stop the spread of AIDS with condom distribution. They actually believe they can stop violence by writing more gun control laws, that more money will fix our public schools, that Foreign Policy means apologizing for America's strength and shaking hands a lot, and that all domestic problems exist because the government simply hasn't spent enough money to solve those problems. All problems treated with the teacup approach mimic the Energizer Bunny. They just keep growing and growing and growing!

The Teacup approach to problem-solving has a near irresistible appeal to a Liberal. Teacup fire fighting gives one an immediate feeling of doing something to fight the fire, and it really looks great to anyone who might be watching. The Conservative, on the other hand, will tend to back off, to surrender part of the burning forest, and to build a break with a real chance of stopping the fire.

Liberals seem compelled to try quick fixes to social engineering. Conservatives meanwhile require answers to simple questions like, "What will the consequences of this action be?" and "will these consequences make things better or worse?"

Liberals attempt to solve the problems of the homeless by direct distribution of blankets, money, food, or building bigger shelters. Liberals attempt to become guardians of the homeless, with never any consideration that perhaps the homeless could *learn* to take care of themselves. One group in California actually made a video tape on how to select the best foods from what is available in dumpsters.

Behind most Liberal programs to deal with the homeless is a belief that, "They can't take care of themselves, therefore I must." A result of that kind of "help" is that the welfare state grows while the human will or need to survive diminishes.

It is most likely that during the past decades the very best place in the world to be homeless was Sweden. The Swedes, enjoying the national prosperity of their labor, decided to take care of the unfortunate homeless people in their nation. At first the programs were a grand success. The work ethic of the people, combined with their individualism, made a state where it was shameful for anyone to admit helplessness, and accept the State's welfare. Then, slowly two things happened: the pride of the people diminished, and gradually, but steadily, more and more people decided to claim their "entitlements." The second thing that occurred was the steady growth of the burden of a Welfare State, being carried by hard-working Swedes. It is not uncommon today for a middle-class Swede to pay over seventy percent of his income in taxes. In some cases the tax laws have grown so absurd that certain people are taxed on 110 percent of their income. Sweden is just now attempting to extricate itself from the horrible, unworkable mess of Socialism.

As Nations around the world attempt to wriggle out of socialistic traps, American Liberals can't seem to get enough of it. U.S. News and World Report estimates that there are over 10,000 Marxist professors teaching in Universities in America today. Marxism sounds wonderful, but it never has and never will work for the betterment of a Nation. People need to ask what consequences will arise before they embrace new "Programs." The American Welfare system was a grand idea, but today only seven percent of the people in America on welfare are working, truly looking for work, or being trained to work.

A discussion of the homeless began one day on my radio program. I really didn't know enough about the situation to talk about it. The only thing I did know is that I felt pain every time I saw someone pan-handling. I really wondered if the greatest nation in history has been reduced to a state where good men stand on street corners with resumés written on cardboard that simply say, "Will work for food." I did what all good broadcasters do. I took my portable microphone, and I went to talk to the "Homeless."

My survey certainly will never qualify as scientific research, but I did find that Liberal giveaways, short of adopting those scruffy-looking fellows, only make the problems worse. I truly challenge you to try to find a "homeless" person who isn't trying to con somebody out of something. They exist, but they are rare. Here are my findings:

- Of the people advertising, "Will work for food" not one actually would work for food, or for that matter, money.
- Most of the "homeless" make about $15.00 an hour begging. Some of the "homeless" were begging in the parking lots of businesses where employees were paid minimum wage, about three-and-a-half times less than the "homeless" made.
- Many of the "homeless" were addicted to alcohol or other drugs, and begged for money only until they had accumulated enough for a fix.
- Some "homeless" begged all day, and at the end of their day, they walked a few blocks to drive away in nice cars.

The plight of the homeless is not a simple matter to address. I also met a family whose car had broken down, were broke, and I believe, truly deserving of help. I introduced that family to a man who does a pretty good job of identifying people who need, and deserve help. Perhaps the true tragedy of the homeless is not that the few who genuinely want and need help are thrown in with a sea of con artists, but the fact that a sea of con artists exists in America. Those con artists are there because some well intentioned Liberals decided one day that throwing a couple of tons of money in the general direction of the homeless would solve their problems. I believe that Liberals are either extremely shortsighted, or they value being seen dealing with problems much more than they do really solving those problems.

Definitions

I took a trip to my local library and looked up the definitions of Liberals and Conservatives. I used those gigantic library editions, and found that *Random House* Second Edition paints a very lovely picture of Liberalism. It was in the *Webster's* Third Edition of the New International that I found the most biting incitements of Liberalism. I'll update the following dictionary terms using illustrations so graciously supplied by Liberals in their natural habitat, and Conservatives waiting for them to self-destruct.

Liberals

"Favorable to progress or reform as in political or religious affairs." (Webster's)

Remember the Clinton Presidential Campaign? How many times did you hear the word "change" spoken and cheered? Do you also recall that nobody spent much time explaining the exact nature of the "change."

This is very simple, readers. The problem with endorsing change for change's sake, is that you might select a change that makes things a lot worse.

"Change In Religious Affairs" (Webster's) is a concept that makes many Liberals salivate with sheer excitement. That's why they get such a kick out of "changing" the words to America to "God shed *her* grace on thee . . . . "(Webster's)

"Favorable to or in accordance with concepts of maximum individual freedom."(Webster's)

Dr. Robert Schuller told a story about school children in New York City. The children came out for recess one day and found the their fence had been taken down to facilitate construction. Just beyond the fence line people hurried by on the sidewalk, and a few feet past the sidewalk was a street filled with fast-moving traffic. The children huddled around the door of their school, and none went near the construction workers who worked busily on the perimeter of the playground.

The behavior of the children lasted for several days, until the fence was restored to its original condition. The children came out for recess and found the fence replaced, and they ran over to it, touched it, and looked as if they were actually hugging their friend, the fence.

People need boundaries. When I worked as a Dormitory Director with very disturbed, court assigned adolescents, I regularly asked those young men to tell me what they wanted from me and my staff. Consistently they told me, "We want you to be more strict." That was a facility with fourteen foot high fences, locked doors everywhere, roving guards, and it wasn't "strict" enough to keep those young men out of trouble. They were locked up because their lives had gotten out of control, and they instinctively knew that boundaries to behavior presented a sane solution to their problems.

Everyone who doesn't enjoy the solitude of a deserted island needs to recognize and respect boundaries. The old cliche about individual freedom is "your freedom extends as far down your arm as you can go without hitting my nose." A society is only as civilized as its people's recognition and respect for the boundaries of human behavior.

Imagine what a positive difference it would make in our nation if men never hit women or children, if people didn't drive while intoxicated, or if children obeyed their parents. Many Liberals actually don't comprehend the need for any behavioral boundaries. They are the type of people who responded to the murder, arson and looting of the Los Angeles riots by demanding amnesty for the rioters. I suppose they perceive murder as the expression of freedom of speech, and arson and looting as alternative lifestyles.

Liberals obviously delight in flaunting their freedoms with an "in your face" attitude that ignores the freedom of others. Absolute freedom without boundaries is chaos.

"Characterized by generosity and a willingness to give."(Webster's)

For more accuracy I suggest changing the word, "give" to "spend other people's money." Have you been able to keep

count of how many of President Clinton's appointees didn't
bother to pay into the social security funds of their servants?
Much Liberal "giving" is of the Robin Hood variety. Liberals want
to give to the poor by taking (stealing through taxation) from the
rich. The result of leveling the incomes of all is the creation of a
Nation of poor people.

"Not bound by traditional ideas or values."(Webster's)

Liberals give fuel to the saying that insanity is doing the
same thing over and over, expecting different results. The current crop of Liberals go far beyond a release from "Traditional
ideas and values." For example, the Clinton Liberals have
either ignored or revised any history texts that contradicted their
beliefs. Liberals today are dedicated to resurrecting the same
brand of atheistic socialism that failed so miserably in Russia,
Cuba, etc. The Liberal's religious belief that they are a "chosen
people" motivates them to attempt precisely what has failed for
so many, for so long.

" . . . excessively free or indecorous in behavior, licentious
. . . ."(Webster's)

The operative word here is not "free," but "excessively." If
you had been given a program for the Clinton inaugural festivi-
ties would you have chosen to attend the Lesbian or the Trans-
vestite's Ball? (Liberals actually deal with stumpers like that.)

" . . . free from restraint or check, unchecked by a sense of
the decorous, the fitting, or the polite . . . ."(Webster's)

"Fitting" and "Polite" are trigger words, guaranteed to get a
rise out of many left-wing activists. "Polite by whose standards?" they demand. Certainly these are offensive words to
people who live life by the one rule creed, "There are no rules."

Homosexuals have confronted me passionately in public
debate over my use of the term "homosexual lifestyle." They
contend that there is no pattern of behavior common to homosexuals. In May 1993, a few hundred thousand homosexuals
held a rally in Washington, and video tapes of their celebrations

were so obscene that the manager of a TV Station that aires my weekly program refused to show the tapes. One Lesbian speaker talked about her desire to have sex with the first lady. Other naked people joined a parade mimicking masturbation and copulation. I call the things people often exhibit "lifestyle."

A Shriner's parade always has men on tiny motorcycles. A Christian parade always features hymns and prayers. A rodeo parade always has horses. A Circus parade isn't a real Circus parade without elephants. A homosexual rally always includes people living down to the lowest expectations of human misbehavior. That is "Unchecked by the fitting or polite."

" . . . lacking moral restraint."(Webster's)

One Air Force General, was relieved of duty because he said that President Clinton was a lying, dope-smoking, womanizing, draft-dodger. The General committed an impropriety. No doubt about that. As improper as his comments were, they were accurate. A week before the 1992 Presidential election I interviewed a former member of Governor Clinton's staff from Arkansas. I began the interview by asking the man what he thought of his former boss. He said, "Bill Clinton is a lying, dope-smoking, womanizing, draft-dodger." Name-calling is crude and inappropriate. The documented, long-term behavioral patterns of a presidential candidate don't amount to name-calling, but to the reporting of news that American voters deserve to know.

In the 1992 election, the Clinton team was so utterly defenseless that they were forced to respond to constant accusations with the "character isn't an issue" defense. The remarkable thing is not that the president showed no moral restraint, but that forty-three percent of the American voters didn't care.

" . . . not confined or restricted to the exact or the literal . . ." (Webster's)

One evening I attended a meeting of a group in a study program called, *A Course In Miracles*. I went to the meeting at the suggestion of a friend. After the meeting I asked my friend about some of the things that had been said at the meeting. I asked, "Don't you think its strange that those people claim to be God?" My friend answered, "Oh, that's what they say, but its not really what they mean." I then asked her if when they prayed to a "father, mother, sister, brother, God" had they identified any of that polytheistic group? My friend said, that the *Course In Miracles* people were really praying to Christ, and acknowledging all of the aspects of God's personality. Predictably, my next question was, "Why don't they just say what they mean?"

Liberals are not bound by the "literal or the exact." Disposing of the meaning of words gives the people who said the words the ability to change the meaning. Liberals, when confronted by unwanted facts (History), simply rewrite the facts (Revisionism). Consider Oliver Stone's version of the J.F.K. Assassination. There were obviously a lot of people Mr. Stone didn't like, so he revised the history of the assassination, and implicated all the people he didn't like and several other names and agencies taken from the Washington, D.C. phone book.

Conservatism

" . . . disposed to preserve existing conditions, institutions, to limit change . . . ."(Webster's)

I confess. When Paul McCartney appeared in concert a few blocks from my home I didn't even think of going. (I'm still upset about the break up of the Beatles.)

Conservative allegiance runs deeper than the mere, "If it ain't broken, don't fix it" mentality. Most conservatives believe they really should "dance with the one that brung ya." This mindset can accurately be called loyalty.

"Conservatism run amuck" is the resistance to anything that disrupts existing routine. Management expert Max Weber taught that the three elements of bureaucratic activity are, input, process and output. He warned of the danger of allowing process to become the never-changing element of work. He cited organizations where workers had lost sight of why they did things, and resisted any change because, "This is the way we do things."

Radical conservatism can lead to antiquitization by clinging to routines with minds closed to progress. Lyndon Johnson said that anyone who waited until all the facts are in will be too late to make a difference. "Functioning" means making decisions and taking action. Conservatism without balance can immobilize people, organizations or nations.

Liberalism and Conservatism have both positive and negative points. The key is balance. Conservatism, at its worst is resistance to progress, and clinging to process even if it is counterproductive. Liberalism, at its worst is a great confusion over the difference between progress and change.

Conservatives respect absolutes, and the radical Liberalism of the '90s puts absolutes as reliable as the word of God under attack. The radical Liberals of today have elevated diversity to the sacramental level, and their acceptance of anything and everything is diametrically opposed to the Conservative respect for certain never-changing absolutes.

The silliness of modern Liberals is exposed in their inconsistencies. They proclaim that they are tolerant for all people, regardless of race, creed, color, sexual orientation, etc. They then attack Christians at every opportunity. The problem is, of course, that Liberals aren't bound by the literal or the exact. (Translation: They don't mean what they say.)

Chapter 4

Coup dé Tat

In 1972, I was an Intelligence Analyst at the U.S. Army Headquarters in Heidelberg, Germany. My supervisor had me read a book titled, *Coup dé Tat*. The book was a guide for anyone who wanted to take over a nation. My supervisor's intentions were clear. He wanted me to begin to think like the enemy, to get inside the heads of some of the world's anarchists. Analyzing intelligence is much like a game. In step one we surmise what steps would indicate a major military or political change in a country. In step two we diligently look for any of those indicators, and in step three we analyze and report on those indicators.

Recently I have "played" a variation of "the game." In this variation, I ask myself what would be the indicators of a takeover of my own country. The results of the game were frightening. What follows is a brief summary of an imaginary "battle plan:"

If, about thirty years ago, a group of people had wanted to destroy America, they might have drawn up a plan. If that imaginary group of people contained military and political genius, the following is what their battle plan might have looked like. Each point of the plan to cripple America is indicated in bold print. In regular print I summarize what has already been done to implement "The Plan."

Step One:
Destroy the Nation's Belief in God:

Theologian, Hans Kung, wrote about the "Death of God" theology, and of how "militant-aggressive atheism" was essential to the rise of Soviet Socialism. I distinctly remember the Nuns in elementary school evoking fear and pity for the peoples of Russia who weren't allowed to worship God. At the time I thought that the Communist Rulers were as barbaric as any savage hoard who had ever walked the earth. Militant-aggressive atheism today is a core belief, and a mighty cause of the radical Left.

The move to remove God from American life began in 1962. In two cases heard by the U.S. Supreme court the rights of children to pray together in school was essentially removed. In Abington School District vs. Shempp:

The Schempp Family challenged a Pennsylvania statue that provided that, " . . . At least ten verses from the Holy Bible shall be read, without comment, at the opening of each public school on each school day. Any child shall be excused from the Bible reading, or attending such Bible reading upon the written request of his parent or guardian."

In the companion case to the Schempp case, Madalyn Murray, who by a second marriage became Madalyn Murray O'Hair, initiated Murray vs. Curlett, challenging the right to pray in the Baltimore public schools. The Schempp-Murray suit, in effect, was the militant-aggressive atheist action that took God out of the public schools in America. The Schempp family regularly attended the Unitarian Church, while Madalyn Murray O'Hair became head of the America Atheist Center in Austin, Texas. Mrs. Murray O'Hair's son, William, later became a born again Christian, and took out newspaper ads, apologizing for his mother's part in the infamous suit.

It is interesting to note that the bellicose, bullying tactics of the anti-God movement in America have been carried out almost exclusively by the American Civil Liberties Union, the ACLU. (Justice Felix Frankfurter, a supporter of the majority decision in the Schempp-Murray suit, was also a founding father of the ACLU.)

Justice Tom Clark was chosen to write the opinion of the Supreme Court in this suit. He chose to make his case by quoting a letter written by Roger Williams to the town of Providence, some 300 years earlier. The quotes from Williams read:

"There goes many a ship to sea, with many hundreds of souls in one ship, whose weal and woe is common, and is a true picture of a commonwealth, or a human combination, or society. It hath fallen out sometimes, that both Baptists and Protestants, Jews and Turks, may be embarked in one ship; upon which supposal, I affirm that all the liberty of conscience I ever pleaded for, turns upon these two hinges, that none of the Baptists, Protestants, Jews, or Turks be forced to come to the ship's prayers or worship, nor compelled from their own particular prayers or worship, if they practice any."

Judge Clark omitted the sentence that follows the words he quoted from Roger William's letter. That sentence reads:

"I further add. That I never denied, that notwithstanding this liberty, the commander of this ship ought to command the ship's course, yea, and also command that justice, peace and sobriety, be kept and practiced, both among the seamen and all the passengers."

When you examine the complete text of Roger Williams you can see that he relates non-mandatory prayer with "Justice, Peace And Sobriety." Without God, there is no "Justice, peace and sobriety." Without God, Chaos is guaranteed.

In the Bible in several places, God speaks explicitly about what happens when a generation turns it back on its Creator. Whenever a generation turns its back on God, then God will turn His back on their nation. Jeremiah 8:3 says: *Whenever I banish them all the survivors of this evil nation will prefer death to life, declares the Lord.*

There is very strong evidence that America has been suffering the literal wrath of God since we turned our back on Him through the Supreme Court rulings of 1962.

In the few years following 1962, we saw the assassination of President Kennedy, the involvement in the longest and most unpopular war we ever fought as a Nation, the deterioration of law and order, and the beginning of what is now obviously a nationwide reversal of morals and values. As we watch the evening News tonight or read the newspaper we can see the wisdom of Roger Williams who linked prayer with the maintenance of *justice, peace and sobriety.*

Step Two:
With God Removed,
Offer the People a New God,
the Central Government

In Pat Robertson's book, *The Secret Kingdom*, he warns against turning to a false god. He then suggests that the most popular new "god" in America is the central government.

Before his election, Mr. Bill Clinton portrayed himself as a moderate. Many thought that the moderate facade was a cover-up for a radical, left-wing Liberal. To some, Clinton's politics go far beyond Liberalism, and are truly Socialist.

When asked to name the two people he most admired, Mr. Clinton named Nelson Mandela and Gorbachev. No one expected him to name biblical heroes such as King David or Peter. He might have named American Heroes like Washington or Lincoln. It was no surprise to me that he named a Russian Communist, a staunch champion of communism, as a personal hero, and Mr. Mandela, the author of *How to Be a Good Communist.*

Embracing Socialism means clinging to the intellectual, militant-aggressive atheist theories that have never worked anywhere for anyone. This is precisely the sort of theoretical nonsense that can be expected from a man who squandered a Rhodes Scholarship to Oxford and demonstrated against his own Country in the streets of London while supporting the immoral and ungodly leadership of the maniacal Ho Chi Minh.

Before you dismiss this warning of the development of a Socialist America, please read a few quotations from these men who are considered brilliant by so many socialists.

In December 1847 and January 1848 Karl Marx and Frederick Engels wrote the *Communist Manifesto*. Here are some samples of their "Brilliance."

On Ownership of Private Property:

"The distinguishing feature or communism is not the abolition of property generally, but the abolition of bourgeois property. But the modern bourgeois private property is the final and most complete expression of the system of producing and appropriating products, that is based on class antagonisms, on the exploitation of the many by the few.

"In this sense, the theory of the Communists may be summed up in the single sentence: Abolition of Private Property."

Does this sound familiar, America? Does this smack of what Mr. Clinton said during his campaign about how the rich deserved to be heavily taxed?

There's More!

"On the Family" Abolition of the Family!

"Even the most radical flare up at this infamous proposal of the Communists.

On what foundation is the present family, the bourgeois family based? On capital, on private gain. In its completely developed form this family exists only among the bourgeoisie. But this state of things finds its complement in the practical absence of the family among the proletarians, and in public prostitution."

(When I read these lines of Marx and Engels demanding to know the basis of the family, I wanted to shout out to their ignorant ghosts, "It's in the Bible, and if you hadn't censored that great document you would know the answer to your stupid question.")

On Separating Children From the Influence of Their Parents:

"Do not charge us with wanting to stop the exploitation of children by their parents. To this crime we plead guilty.

But you will say we destroy the most hallowed of relations, when we replace home education by social.

And your education! Is not that also social, and determined by the social conditions under which you educate."

(This rhetoric sounds remarkably like some of the things you might hear at a National Education Association Convention today.)

On the Communist Rulers as God:

"The charges against Communism made from a religious, a philosophical, and generally from an ideological standpoint, are not deserving of serious examination . . . . Communism abolishes eternal truths, it abolishes all religion, and all morality, instead of constituting them on a new basis; it therefore acts in contradiction to all past historical experience."

(If people had not embraced these rantings, they would be laughable. (Remember, you are reading a list of things to do to destroy America.) Marx and Engels wrote a similar list in their *Communist Manifesto*. The frightening thing is that this wackiness sounds remarkably like the rhetoric of modern American Clintonites. This is the game plan according to Marx and Engels.)

- "Abolition of property in land and application of all rents of land to public purposes. (Robin Hood economy.)

- A heavy progressive or guaranteed income tax. (The stimulus package?)
- Abolition of all right of inheritance. (Consistent with the development of national dependency.)
- Confiscation of the property of all emigrants and rebels.
- Centralization of credit in the hands of the State, by means of a National Bank with State Capitol and an exclusive monopoly. (The Federal Reserve?)
- Centralization of the means of communication and transport in the hands of the State. (The "Fairness Doctrine" to control the content of radio programs.)
- Extension of factories and instruments of production owned by the State; the bringing into civilization of waste-lands, and the improvement of the soil generally in accordance with a common plan. (Subsidized Farming.)
- Equal liability of all to labor. Establishment of industrial armies, especially for agriculture.
- Combination of agriculture with manufacturing industries; gradual abolition of the distinction between town and country, by a more equable distribution of the population over the country. (They want to be able to tell you where to live.)
- Free education for all children in public schools. Abolition of children's factory labor in its present form. Combination of education with industrial production." (This sounds like the NEA to me.)

A translation of these ten points is that under communism you are owned by the almighty, all-knowing State. The State tells what you can have and what you can't have, how to raise and educate your children, when and how much money you can have and how you can spend it. The State makes all decisions for everyone.

Is the Clinton government leading this nation into a quagmire similar to the debacle of Soviet Socialism? You answer that question yourself. Answer that question as you hear Hillary Clinton subtly inform America that her new Health Care Plan will include funding for abortions (which is illegal because of the Hyde Amendment). Listen and decide for yourself as more and more of your freedoms dissolve while the government assumes more and more responsibility for how you will live your life. Listen. Watch. Decide. Just don't take too long about your responsibility. Every single time you accept the government's invitation to take care of you, you surrender more of your personal freedom.

<h2 align="center">Step Three:
Target the Most Vulnerable Segment
of the Population, the Young.</h2>

In California, two brothers are tried for murdering their wealthy parents, and going on a spending spree with their inheritance. Their defense is that their parents abused them. In Florida a 12-year-old boy sues his parents for divorce. He wins.

Where will it end? Will your daughter someday press charges when you tell her she can't go to the mall? Couldn't she charge you with restriction of her freedom? Planned Parenthood, a leader in the Abortion Industry, advertises with a radio announcement, that they are ready to talk to you when your parents won't listen. Will you someday be charged with invasion of privacy when you attempt to find out what the wonderful folks at Planned Parenthood are telling your daughter about abortion?

In 1971, I sat in a classroom and listened to a Boston University Professor teaching a graduate course in Educational Counseling. The professor claimed to have touched on a concept that held the very key to the future of Education in America. He resisted coming out and telling us about his stroke of genius, and built us all up for the big announcement like a hawker on one of those TV Infomercials. Finally the grand moment arrived and he announced that *tolerance for ambiguity* was the great hope for American education.

I am certain now that the professor had confused the solution to American educational problems with a three word formula for being accepted by NEA. There is so much ambiguity in American schools, and throughout American society that young people don't know right from wrong. For the past thirty years parents and teachers have been using the great cop-out, tolerating all ambiguity as if it were a contest to see how much foolishness we could tolerate. The "tolerance for ambiguity" crowd have succeeded in the total elimination from the vocabularies of the Politically Correct words like succeed, fail, good, bad, and ultimately right and wrong.

There is great cunning in the plan. The NEA, with the help of confederates like the ACLU and Planned Parenthood, have driven a wedge between parents and their children. The exposed young minds are just waiting to be filled with liberal doctrine, as our nation is herded toward Socialism. These products of an ambiguous environment mature and are elevated to positions of leadership as high as the position of U.S. President.

Step Four:
Invert Values

I spoke at an anti-drug rally in a football stadium. I made a teaching aid to help me make an important point. I cut a large triangle out of wood. On the triangle I painted what I called a *Pyramid of Values*. My pyramid looked like this:

—Drugs—
———Job———
————Country————
—————Family—————
——————God——————

I then talked about what happens when the tiny value of "I will try drugs" is added to the very top of the pyramid. In some cases the initial experimentation can lead quickly to *Addiction*. In the addicted state, obtaining and using the drug of choice becomes the primary or base value. This predicates the absurd situations where mothers prostitute themselves for drugs, where fathers commit murder for drugs, where all of the previously important values in a person's life are, all of a sudden, secondary to obtaining drugs. I illustrated this point by inverting the pyramid, leaving all values balanced precariously on the value of obtaining and using drugs:

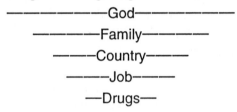

```
—————————God—————————
————————Family—————————
————————Country—————————
—————Job—————
——Drugs——
```

The values of our entire nation are being inverted, turned upside down, and in some cases, the values that made our nation great are simply being discarded.

I watched the finals of the Miss Texas contest on TV. The beautiful, young women were being asked randomly selected questions. One especially animated young woman was asked what she would do if she and her husband were poor, and she found a wallet with $1,000 and all of the appropriate ID. Without hesitation she exclaimed, "I'd keep it. If we needed that money, I'd keep it." The audience applauded in approval. I was dumbfounded. Not only had the contestant said that she would steal someone else's money because she needed it, but the audience was carrying on like they had just heard a swell idea. Don't look now, America, but our values, our understanding of right and wrong is completely warped. Criminals rape and kill, and their victims are ignored while society finds it intolerable that those poor, little ole criminals felt so awful that they had to do those things. In a recent poll, twenty-five percent of high school children said they had cheated on tests, and would lie on a resumé in order to get a job. Rioters loot, murder, attack innocent people, and set fires, and their pastors show up the next day telling the world it was justified because of an inattentive society.

One night I was on a panel discussing the pros and cons of homosexual privilege in the military. I was on the side opposing the Clinton promotion of homosexuality. The debate became heated, and one man countered something said about God's Law as he blurted out, "God is good, therefore there is no right and there is no wrong." I suppose that means that a good God wouldn't have rules. That is a very popular and most *Politically Correct* view of values. It is also a method that I can guarantee can and will destroy any great nation.

Step Five:
Destroy the Nation's Heritage

Who discovered America? I was taught over forty years ago that the answer to that question was Christopher Columbus. Columbus had three major things working against him as far as the politically correct were concerned:

1. He was a white guy from Europe.
2. He actually was in it for the money, working for profit.
3. He, was one of those doggoned Christians, and he prayed on the way, after he arrived, and even preached to the natives.

As a rule, the Politically Correct Revisionists cannot stand anyone who is white, capitalist and Christian. When the Revisionists don't like a person or event from history, they merely rewrite the history. So Columbus was *reinvented* (Does that term sound familiar?) Columbus went from "The Father of Our Country" to the villainous exploiter of the natives, the despot who ravaged our continent, etc.

Making heros into villains, and visa versa is an easy chore for modern revisionists. Anyone who can analyze a mob riot and proclaim the looters to be the champions over an oppressive society, after the L.A. Riots, can make quick work out of demonizing Columbus, Washington, Lincoln, et.al.

Step Six:
Give the People Someone or
Something to Blame and to Hate

Many American sports fans delight in giving you the name of the shortstop who blew a World Series, or the Quarterback who lost the Super Bowl. We Americans have a near obsession with identifying and lambasting scapegoats.

Psychologically blaming someone for all of your problems allows people to escape the big R-Word, *Responsibility*. The opposite of taking responsibility for our mistakes is *Finding Someone To Blame*.

The Blame Game has three distinct steps:

1. Whenever accused of doing something wrong, find someone else to blame.
2. If someone else is to blame, then it's not your fault.
3. If it's your fault then you have no responsibility.

The blame game extends to some really absurd situations. Rapists blame their parents saying, "I was abused, so I had to become an abuser."

Women murder their husbands, and blame the dead man for their action.

Children murder their parents, and blame the dead for their action.

A mob of people riot, and blame the jury in a trial miles away from the riot.

A coward dodges the draft while his country is at war, and he blames the government.

Remember Flip Wilson? Whenever he was caught doing something silly or wrong he exclaimed, "The Devil made me do it!" That phrase always got Flip a laugh. The humor was in his desperation to find someone to blame for his problems. When he exhausted his list of people to blame, he could always hang the wrap on "The Devil."

The problem with always blaming someone else for our problems is that the blame goes round and round, and nobody ever takes any responsibility.

I respect one man on Mr. Clinton's cabinet. That man is Henry B. Cisneros. When Mr. Cisneros was the Mayor of San Antonio he was caught having an affair. That was during a time when many American Political Leaders had been caught in similar circumstances, and not a single one of those men had taken responsibility for their cheating. Mayor Cisneros did something radically different. He called a press conference, admitted what he had been doing, and apologized to everyone involved. The story died over night. When a man makes a mistake and then says;

> I did it,
> It was wrong,
> I apologize,

he is publicly taking responsibility. Taking responsibility effectively ends the news worthiness of most events.

I am certainly not condoning promiscuity by a married man. I am saying that I found forgiveness an easy chore because of the way the man took responsibility for his mistake. Compare Mr. Cisneros' behavior with the "I didn't inhale" brand of tap-dancing done by Mr. Clinton, as he was confronted by his draft-dodging, womanizing, dope-smoking and lying. In each instance he piled more and more lies onto his original folly.

I have been doing therapy with addicts for over twenty years. A composite of those therapy sessions might sound like this:

Patient: My husband makes me drink.

Me: Horse feathers!

Patient: Huh?

Me: Nobody makes you drink.

Patient: You don't know my husband.

Me: Are you telling me that your husband holds you down, holds the bottle upside down in your mouth, and pours it in you?

Patient: No, but he makes me drink.

Me: Horse feathers!

          (The patient then starts crying, and finds a new person to blame. Me! She says,)

Patient: Why are you so mean to me? You have been picking on me since the first time I saw you.

Me: I'm not picking on you. It's probably seems that way though.

Patient: It sure does.

Me: That's because I want you to look at the truth in your life.

Patient: My friends all agree that my husband makes me drink.

Me: Your drinking friends?

Patient: Yes, but what does that have to do with it?

Me: It has everything to do with your disease. A symptom of Alcoholism is blaming and shaming. Your drinking friends are all eager to go into "cahoots" with you. If you guys comfort each other, it makes you all more comfortable with your denial.

Patient: I don't like this.

Me: Of course you don't, because I am suggesting
           you give up one of your secondary addictions.

Patient: What is that?

Me: Blaming other people for you problems. You
           are just as addicted to blaming others as you
           are to alcohol.

Patient: I hate this.

Me: I can imagine. Before you give up though,
           let me tell you how important it is for you to
           stop blaming other people for your addiction.

Patient: Go ahead.

Me: As long as you blame others you are not
           taking responsibility. If you keep believing that
           your husband makes you drink, then you will
           have to wait for him to stop drinking for you.

Patient: Say that again.

Me: Your husband doesn't make you drink. You
           decide to drink. If you ever fully accept that
           you are ready to begin your recovery. When
           you accept responsibility for your drinking,
           and only then, you will be ready to take
           responsibility for your sobriety.

Patient: What about God? You always talk about how
           God has to be part of my recovery.

Me: Absolutely, but even God requires that you
           take responsibility for your addiction, and for
           your recovery. God wants you to succeed, but
           even your loving Heavenly Father will not
           stop drinking for you. He will help you in ways
           you have never imagined, but as far as I
           know, God has never yet snatched a bottle

away from someone who wanted to abuse
alcohol.

Just in case you miss the point of my telling you about a
hypothetical therapy session, I believe that much of our Nation
suffers from the same malaise as the woman in my anecdote.
As long as we are intent on blaming others for our problems we
are spiritually immobilized. Progress can only occur when we
claim our mistakes, and subsequently claim responsibility for
their correction.

The Top Three politically correct groups to blame and to
hate are:

1. Conservative–Republicans, (Reagan-Bush years are
   destined to become comparable to the Great
   Depression or the Black Plague in revisionist history).
2. Rich People, (more accurately defined as anyone
   making more money than you make).
3. Christians, (those right-wing fanatics who believe
   the unborn are human, that parents have dominion
   over their children, that homosexuality is wrong and
   all of those other weird ideas).

Worthy of *honorable mention* among the politically-correct
groups to blame and to hate are:

- White guys, (who are ultimately to blame for all of the
  problems of all nonwhite guys).
- Men, (no comment needed about those rascals).
- The educated, (who make the illiterate feel inferior).
- Our parents, (who got the world into this mess).
- Cops, (This author believes police officers are the new
  Vietnam Vets, fighting a war nobody wants, with ill
  defined objectives, while being ridiculed by the public).

Step Six:
Separate the People Into Groups, and
Drive Deep Wedges Between the Groups

Some of the most vindictive writing you will ever find was written by the fathers of Soviet Communism. Marx and Engels fully understood that the working people (proletariat) would never have true unity until they focused on the overthrow of the rich (bourgeois). Whenever they wrote of the bourgeois they communicated as if they were describing some highly contagious scum on the heel of their boots.

Dividing people into groups is an extension of the blaming and hating game. Division in America today is, for many people, the primary means of self identity, that is, people define who they are by who or what they hate.

Some of the most easily recognizable group conflicts in America today are:

Rich	vs.	Poor
White	vs.	Black
Men	vs.	Women
Heterosexual	vs.	Homosexual
Educated	vs.	Illiterate
Parents	vs.	Children
Criminal	vs.	Cops
Christian	vs.	Pagans
Old	vs.	Young
Environmentalists	vs.	Industrialists
Smokers	vs.	Anti-Smokers

The most destructive derision in America today for Christians is the vast chasms between Christian denominations. Several valiant efforts have been made to unite Christian voters. Some of the more successful efforts were made by the Pat Robertson and the Christian Coalition, by Jerry Falwell and the

Silent Majority, and by Beverly LaHaye and the Concerned Women for America. As hard as the people behind those organizations worked, none of them succeeded. If the millions of Christians in America voted as if God was in the voting booth with them (which, by the way, He most certainly was) we would not be lead by a man and a woman who openly promoted abortion on demand, Homosexual privilege, children's rights (over their parent's rights), removal of school prayer, etc., etc., as our national leaders.

Interdenominational Nitpicking

George Burns once said that he had two rules for life:
Rule One: Don't sweat the small stuff.
Rule Two: It's all small stuff.

Is it all small stuff? Or does interdenominational nitpicking keep Christians divided? While Christians commit themselves to petty fighting the pagans are taking over the world.

As I reached this point in typing this manuscript my phone rang. It was my friend, Pastor Jim Dixon who had just returned from a non-denominational Christian Rally in El Paso. The theme of the rally was the coming together of Christians, "a time for healing." One speaker said:

"It's time now to apologize for the hurt we have caused one another. We forgot for awhile that we were all the body of Christ, and it's time now for a healing of those feuding segments."

"Segments of the Body of Christ!" If we remember who we are, and what we are truly about on this earth, we will have what St. Augustine described:

- Unity in the essential matters.
- Liberty in the secondary.
- Charity in all matters.

Step Seven:
Take Over the Media

In the book, *Coup dé Tat*, I read that the very first military target in any city should be the Radio Station. Think about that! The military planners didn't assign primary target statues to the police department, to the Mayor's Office, to the Hospital, to the churches but to the Radio Station. The reasoning is faultless. If you can talk to all of the people, and give them your version of what is happening, you can also persuade them to do exactly what you want them to do.

One development brought tremendous empowerment to TV and Radio in America. That development was the installation of air conditioners in most homes in America. Prior to the age of air conditioners people spent a lot of time on front porches. After the air conditioners became common, homes were built without front porches.

I grew up in the South, and the coolest spot in our home was on the porch. A typical evening in our neighborhood, prior to air conditioning, would find over half of the front porches in my neighborhood filled with living people, with families. There were people talking across streets, joining each other for talks in front yards, or visiting on their porches. People knew each other. People talked. The neighborhood, like the family itself, had a personality all its own.

Those people visiting, sharing their problems and their triumphs on hot, summer evenings, didn't know they were hot. They had never experienced the "climate control" of air conditioning. They shrugged off the discomfort, and went on with their visiting.

When the cool air came floating through those stuffy homes, the urge to luxuriate in the cool was irresistible. Overnight the windows were pulled down, and the doors were shut. There should have been a period of national mourning for the loss of the sense of community in the neighborhoods, but the loss was barely noticed. Waiting inside those cool houses was a new friend, a friend more entertaining, and more fun than the neighbors. There were TV sets, the new neighborhood, the national neighborhood, controlled exclusively by a few people who controlled three major networks. Good-bye, people. Hello, cathode ray tube.

I've already suggested a major task in the overthrow of a country is the inversion of morals. With people watching six or seven hours of TV a day, its relatively simple to portray immorality as the norm. As soon as people begin to believe that everyone else is doing it, it is a quick move to their accepting that behavior as their own.

Television has become a forum for the nation's perverts. Daily Donahue, Sally Jesse, et al., provide forums for transvestites, polygamists, sexual sadists, mothers who have sex with their children's friends, children who have sex with their mother's friends, adults who have sex with children, and the list goes on long enough to provide a continuing daily dose of that bilge. Through it all the hosts urge their audiences to have "tolerance" for these people with "alternative lifestyles," and enough of their audiences applaud to make the most vile behavior appear "normal."

The problem is, of course, that many, many people, sitting zombie-like in front of TV sets, derive their values from whatever Donahue, Sally Jesse, and their audiences think is "Okay." With the absence in so many families of responsible parenting, Donahue and Sally Jesse become the Nation's babysitters, and have more to do with teaching values than anyone else in the lives of the TV generation.

The TV, newspapers and magazines seem to be controlled by Liberals. Nowhere was this more apparent than during the 1992 presidential campaign when Conservatives stood by helplessly as the rosy pictures of candidate Clinton were painted and editors and publishers in offices in New York decided what would be reported, and what would be concealed.

Read over that last paragraph, and you might ask where those few Conservatives got their information if the information was so effectively controlled. The answer is that they heard it on the *Radio*.

Radio seems to have been the one source of information that the Liberals failed to control. It has therefore been the place millions of Conservatives and Christians have turned to find out what was really going on in America. It will be impossible to talk about conservative radio's effect on our nation without discussing Rush Limbaugh.

In 1992, I read a transcript of an interview with Rush Limbaugh. It was published in a trade magazine for the radio industry, in an article most of Rush's fans would never read. Rush was quoted as having said that the three most important things about his radio show were entertainment, entertainment and entertainment. I have listened to Rush for three years now, and his show *is* entertaining. Consistently, for three hours everyday, he does what no broadcaster I know of can match. He uses a few canned skits, and a few "update theme songs" just to pace the show, but for the most part Rush simply sits in front of a microphone and keeps millions of people entertained. I could not in my wildest dreams imagine Donahue, Tom Brokaw, or anyone else doing what Rush does, as well as he does it. Chevy Chase is a very funny man, but he was an almost instant failure at being funny every night for about ten minutes of monologue, and Chevy had the advantage of TV to use his visual gags.

I believe in his heart, Rush thinks of himself as more than an entertainer. He is, in fact, a crusader. Rush doggedly persists with his unique style of conservative commentary when no one else in America is doing anything close to what he does.

Rush has opened doors for Conservative Broadcasters to speak the truth all over America. Some of his predecessors have done Rush-type things, but most have failed at being funny, entertaining, and thought provoking at the same time.

Rush does much more than give courage to other broadcasters. He demonstrates to program directors and station owners and managers that there is a vast audience for Conservative talk.

Step Eight:
Elect Bill Clinton as President of the United States

Weeks before the 1992 Presidential Election Mike Ditka, the outspoken coach, then, of the Chicago Bears, said, "If Bill Clinton is elected, it will be the worst thing that has happened to this country in the last 200 years." At the time I thought, "It probably wouldn't be as bad as the Civil War, or the Vietnam War, or The Great Depression. It wouldn't be the worst thing that has happened in 200 years. It certainly would qualify for the top five or ten, but probably not the worst." Now, I wonder if Mike may have had it right the first time. Bill Clinton's election is the worst thing that has happened to America in 200 years. Surprisingly, the most accurate analysis from all of the political analysts in America, came from a feisty football coach.

I believe that the "erosion of values" began as soon as Bill Clinton was nominated as the Presidential Candidate of the Democratic Party. Repeatedly, the man was confronted by his past, and each time he began an inevitable series of lies to evade the truth. As the truth came out, his lies became increasingly preposterous.

Unfortunately for the Democratic Party and for the liberal media, the die was cast when Mr. Clinton was nominated. They had no choice but to back him, and in doing that they all became co-conspirators in his blatant dishonesty.

The media did a splendid job of covering up what Mr. Clinton really was and always had been. I can offer no more blatant an example of how well the media covered for Mr. Clinton than the response to the Special Orders read before the U.S. Congress by Congressman Bob Dornan of California. For nearly a week, Congressman Dornan, and several of his colleagues, all of whom were veterans and some of whom had been Prisoners of War, were broadcast on C-SPAN, telling the world how deceitful Mr. Clinton had been about his leadership in anti-U.S. Protests during the Vietnam years. I was so impressed with Congressman Dornan's presentation that I took copious notes, bought TV air time from the local cable company, summarized Representative Dornan's presentation down into an hour, and went on the air with the story. At the same time the depths of deceit Mr. Clinton had employed and was employing to cover his past never became a major story. Attempts to expose the man for his immense lack of character was met with the now infamous cry of "Character isn't an issue."

If the character, or lack of character, of a man nominated to lead his nation isn't an issue, then that country is in serious trouble, very serious trouble. Have you ever thought about how incredibly stupid it is to say about a man, "Character isn't an issue." That, in effect, means, "I don't care if the man lies, just listen to how good he sounds."

The greatest threat to America's future lies in the fact that America, as a whole, has a memory of no more than six weeks. The Clinton people have broken numerous promises, and been more radical in their liberal administration of the government than most Americans suspected. The real horror is that America will forget the broken promises, and allow itself again to be seduced by lies.

Step Nine:
Trivialize Human Life

One million, six hundred thousand babies are killed every year in America. Hillary Clinton's Health Care Package seeks to make those murders a federally-funded project. The murders are trivialized by calling the babies tissue masses.

This is one former viable tissue mass who sees the atrocity for what it is, and insists on calling abortion what it is, murder. When dealing with the Politically Correct, it is very important to insist on calling things by their correct names. If, for example, we call a baby a tissue mass, it makes it more palatable to abortionists who clamp, mash, hammer or suffocate the life out of those "tissue masses." If we call murder abortion, it suddenly isn't a crime. If we accept Dr. Jack Kevorkian's new word for a doctor killing his patients, "medicide," then it even sounds like a legitimate medical procedure. (In this book, I will call things what they actually are.)

Two years ago I interviewed the New Mexico Director of the Right To Life Organization on my radio program. The news was full of accounts of how Dr. Jack Kevorkian had murdered his patients. The newspapers, of course, called the doctor's work, Doctor-Assisted Suicide. This really is a non-distinction. What is to prevent anyone from killing anyone else, and deny that they were murdering the person, but assisting in their suicide? I asked the Right To Life Director, "Why do Americans have this interest, all of a sudden, in killing sick people?"

Without an instant's hesitation she replied, "Because of the continuing promotion of abortion in our country. As people become more and more comfortable with killing of the unborn, they become jaded and apathetic about the killing of other groups."

That lady made a lot of sense to me. If we can change the status of an unborn baby to a tissue mass and murder that

infant, why can't we make other changes to facilitate murder.
Changes like:

Old People	to	The Terminally Ill
Sick People	to	The Incurable
Retarded People	to	Permanently Impaired
Non-Compliants	to	Permanent Misfits
Non-Believers	to	Non-Compliant

One Issue Voters Unite!

During the 1992 Presidential Campaign I received a telephone call from a listener who told me that Ross Perot was entering the race for President (the first time). I was instantly excited. I knew what Ross Perot had done in Texas with the Texas War On Drugs, and what he had done for Vietnam Vets, and what kind of a successful business he ran. Ross Perot sounded to me like exactly like the kind of man America needed. The next day I learned that Ross and his wife were supporters of Planned Parenthood, and that they favored easy access to abortion. Thus ended my twenty-two hour support for Ross Perot as President.

I explained why I thought an enthusiastic pro-abortion candidate was no candidate, and I said it on the air. My next call was from an angry man who demanded to know how I could, in good conscience, make a decision on a man's capability to be president on a single issue. That was a very good question, almost as good as the answer I gave that caller.

If a man has little or no respect for human life, especially the most defenseless of human beings, then what on earth will that man respect?

Insisting on a pro-life candidate is much more than a one-issue approach to voting. Underlying a person's view of abortion, is a revelation of exactly how that person views human life. If the view of human life is a trivial one, then that person certainly is not qualified to be the Commander-in-Chief of the

Armed Forces, and make life and death decisions about our service men and women.

Step Ten:
Make Political Correctness
the Unwritten, But Accepted, Law

Who determines the law of the land? Is it the people? The local judges? The Supreme Court? Or, is law determined by Political Correctness? When the Los Angeles Police Officers accused of beating Rodney King were acquitted, a riot ensued. The response to the riot was to try the officers a second time. When the same people who rioted began to menace the officials conducting the trials of those accused of beating Reginald Denny, the accused were acquitted.

I did not attend and listen to all of the evidence in any of those trials. However, I did notice that after the riots all of the verdicts were *Politically Correct.* My questions about who determines law in the Country are not rhetorical. I am not certain if our nation is governed by the courts, or by some cockeyed view of what is or is not *Politically Correct.*

The major problem with using Political Correctness to govern behavior is that Political Correctness is consistently inconsistent. The very same people who demand freedom of speech for everyone, and will go the limit for some rap artist to rap about killing cops, will bring suit against a six year-old who wants to talk about the Birth of Christ in a public school. The only recognizable common thread to Political Correctness is that it is consistently anti-Christian and immoral.

Madonna is a self-proclaimed high priestess of the Politically Correct. In defense of her pornographic book, *Sex,* she said she was liberating young people from their hangups about sex. On the surface, Madonna is a champion of tolerance, accepting anything that anyone chooses to do. Right? Wrong.

The same Madonna who would have us all believe that sexual perversion is chic, had some things to say about fat people. Madonna said, "Fat is a big problem for me. It sets off something in my head that says 'overindulgent pig.'" When people become tolerant for pedophilia, but believe that obesity is animalistic, they have become selectively tolerant. (Translation: *Selective tolerance* is intolerance.)

Chapter 5

Politically Correct Lies (PCLs) and Doses Of Truth (DOTs)

Word Byte Combat

Because political correctness is communicated by the media, the official language of Political Correctness is Word Byte. The Politically Correct attempt to silence the truth with a word, phrase or a few sentences on every subject. The bad news is that these word byte salvos from the enemy are written and broadcast so often that they become quite effective. The good news is that they are all lies, and can be blown away with a DOT.

In this chapter, I have included the twenty-five most popular and politically correct word bytes. With each PCL word byte, I supply a DOT. The PCLs and DOTs in this chapter can be valuable to either liberals or conservatives. The Liberals can recite the PCLs anytime on the Donahue show and receive applause from a hundred or so New Yorkers (Synonymous in most cases with liberals.) The Conservatives can use the DOTs just in case their children bring home PCLs. (I'm sure you don't want those things in your home.)

The PCL About My Manners

PCL #1

Marvin, you are disrespectful of the President. You avoid calling him President Clinton, and always refer to him as Mr. Bill or Mr. Bill Clinton.

DOT #1

Whoa, there! I am not blazing new trails of disrespect, but merely following the lead of our leader. During the 1992 campaign he always referred to my President as either Mr. Bush or simply, Bush. I refer to Mr. Clinton as President Clinton when I say Mass, and during Mass I always pray for President Clinton and for his wife Hillary.

PCLs About Families

PCL #2

Conservatives, and especially Christians, want to restrict the definition of families to a married man and woman raising children. That leaves people like Lesbians and Homosexuals who want to adopt "out in the cold."

DOT #2

The married man and woman model is indeed our ideal. The fact is that single parent families happen, and our Nation's churches are filled with them. Meanwhile, you want to redefine the family as warm-blooded mammals sharing rent. Homosexual and Lesbian couples can never co-create naturally, and isn't "natural" one of the liberals favorite criteria for value?

PCL #3

Parents can't, nor should they, try to make their children do what they (parents) want.

DOT # 3

The family was never meant to be a democracy, but a Kingdom, under a King and Queen (Mom and Dad.) Their job descriptions (See Ephesians 6:1–4) include, . . . *bring them up in the training and instruction of the Lord.*

PCL #4

Parents who smoke dope with their children, allow them to have sex at home, and allow them to do everything and to have everything, get to be great pals with their children.

DOT #4

Parenting isn't about being a pal, but leading, teaching and nurturing.The child who enjoys growing up with a pal will inevitably resent what the parents do not teach. (Translation: it really does all come around, and any of life's lessons you skip will have to be learned the hard way.)

PCL #5

There is no hope for America because Fathers have not been taking responsibility.

DOT #5

You have identified the problem, the failure of so many American Fathers. You are too pessimistic about the hope. A national movement is afoot, led by organizations like The Promise Keepers and 100 black men. These men are putting Fathers back where they belong, into the leadership roles of their families. The American Family is in crisis, but the "fat lady" hasn't even warmed up yet.

PCLs About Drugs

PCL #6

Tobacco and alcohol cause more deaths than any other drugs in America, so why not legalize pot.

DOT #6

You have a half truth. If tobacco and alcohol were introduced to the FDA today, they would never be legalized. We made a mistake. Lets not make more mistakes. If I had rattlesnakes in my yard, I wouldn't bring in copperheads because I already had snakes.

PCL #7

Over 80 percent of our prison population are in prison for drug crimes. If we freed them we'd immediately solve our prison crowding problem.

DOT #7

The optimum word is "related" as in "Drug-related crimes." The drug subculture is filled with ruthless people who think nothing of murder, robbery, extortion, arson, etc. Most of those 80 percent are exactly where they belong. If, however, they ever are all released at once, I will suggest they move onto your cul-de-sac.

PCLs About Abortion

PCL #8

Abortion is about a woman's right to choose what she does with her body. Its nobody else's business.

DOT #8

Abortion **denies** women the right to choose. Of the 1.6 million annual abortions in America, over half take the lives of an unborn female. These women never have the right to choose anything.

PCL #9

Mr. Marvin, it always seems to me that the people speaking out against abortion are old men like you. You don't have babies, so why do you think this is any of your business.

DOT #9

Okay, my liberal friends. Bring along your crayons as we return to our Freshman biology books. A man contributes half of the ingredients to the divine recipe for creation of a human life. The more men become involved in reproduction and all that follows (parenting) the better off we all will be. Meanwhile you've raised a question I can't answer. Do Lesbians demanding abortions make sense to you?

PCLs About Homosexuality

PCL #l0

Homosexuals are born that way.

DOT #10

With as many homosexual scientists trying so many times to prove that, not one scientific study attempting to prove genetic predisposition to homosexuality has been conclusive.

PCL #11

Homosexuals have a natural right to be parents.

DOT #11

Great! Then let one homosexual couple, unassisted, make a baby. Call me when that happens.

PCL #12

Discriminating against homosexuals is like racism.

DOT #12

Wrong! People are born into a race. Homosexuality is based on behavior, not genetics. No doctor, in no delivery room, ever, has said anything like, "Mrs. Jones, you are the proud mother of a seven and a-half pound, homosexual, boy child."

PCL #13

Homosexuals always have served in the military and they should be allowed to come out of the closet in uniform.

DOT #13

Yup! Homosexuals have served, and often with distinction. However, they have never held parades in front of Post Headquarters during Gay and Lesbian Pride Week. Military service is synonymous with conformity in behavior. Flaunting homosexuality has never been described in any service manual as acceptable military behavior. So long as it does not contribute to the accomplishment of a military mission it should not be authorized.

PCL #14

You only oppose homosexuals because you are homophobic.

DOT #14

In response to your second grade level name calling, I remind you that heterophoria is just as real and probably far more prevalent than homophobia.

PCL #15

Homosexuality is no longer considered a mental disorder by the America Medical Association (AMA).

DOT #15

The AMA decision to take homosexuality, which was previously considered a mental disorder, off its list of disorders was not a unanimous decision, and it was made in reaction to intense homosexual political maneuvering. Homosexuality is not recognized by the AMA as a disorder, but it is not a happy life, and certainly not a life that can accurately be called "gay."

PCL #16

AIDS is a heterosexual disease.

DOT #16

Heterosexual AIDS cases are on the rise, especially among females, but the highest at-risk group is still homosexuals. To misconstrue or misrepresent that information is genocide of homosexuals.

PCLs About the Clinton Government

PCL #17

We can give you all free health care.

DOT #17

Two of my friends died from the effects of Agent Orange this year, and both left families suing the VA for support. The VA is an example of government administered "Free" health care. Ask vets about how great their free health care is. The government can't administer the VA or Medicaid without outrageous incompetence, so how can they possibly take over and improve the most complicated industry in our Nation?

PCL #18

Mr. Clinton said, "I want the American People to begin to think of themselves as customers of government."

DOT #18

Why on earth would we ever do that?: I can't think of anything, other than providing for a common defense, that the government can do half as well as the private sector. I would much rather think of myself as an employer of the government than as a customer. I got that radical idea from something I heard one time about, "government of the people, by the people and for the people." Our government was never intended to be "To the people."

PCL #19

Mr. Clinton is our President because the people elected him.

DOT #19

Not really. Mr. Clinton is President because of the people who voted for him, and still believe they voted for Perot.

PCLs About Education and the NEA

PCL # 20

The National Education Association (NEA) opposes school choice because it would allow the Conservatives to re-segregate America's Schools.

DOT #20

Not even close. The NEA opposes school choice because choice would include comparison, and expose the NEA's incompetency. Meanwhile over twenty percent of the NEA members send their own children to private schools.

PCL #21

You Conservatives are always picking on the NEA. We are just a union trying to get more pay and better working conditions for our teachers.

DOT #21

If the NEA is just another union, then Piranha are only fish. They demand more and more money while their incompetence results in over a million high school graduates each year who are functionally illiterate. If the NEA really wanted to educate our kids it would take all of its political lobbyists and emissaries to liberal special interest groups, (Planned Parenthood, the National Organization of Women, ACLU, etc.) and have those people either find other jobs or teach children how to read, write and do math.

PCL #22

Public education has made great strides in raising the self-esteem of American students.

DOT #22

Self-esteem is a false feeling you have created with New Age exercises and teaching. Kids "feel good" about their math ability, but when they get into the market place they discover that they can't add, subtract or multiply. Your so-called self-esteem would be better termed self-deception. At the same time you have been raising self-esteem, SAT scores have dropped 80 points.

PCL #23

Teachers have to teach kids *values clarification* because their parents have failed.

DOT #23

You are half-right. Many parents have failed as leaders of their families. The liberal educational machine, however, is attempting to diminish parental authority and institutionalize liberal morality. (Translation: Liberal morality is immorality.)

PCL #24

Schools should distribute condoms because kids are going to have sex anyway.

DOT #24

Some kids are going to have sex anyway, while others deserve to know that abstinence is the only safe option that really works. Distributing condoms to kids is like giving them bullet-proof vests to stop them from shooting each other.

PCL #25

Why teach abstinence? Kids aren't going to listen to that.

DOT #25

As William Bennett said, "Abstinence works every time its used."

Chapter 6

Politically Correct Patterns of Sexual Misbehavior

Marvin:	Pssst!
Young man:	What?
Marvin:	Interested in some really great sex?
Young man:	Who isn't?
Marvin:	I'm not talking about a quickie, I'm talking the best sex you'll ever have. Guaranteed.
Young man:	Keep talking.
Marvin:	Here is the way it works. You pray, and live your life according to the word of God . . . .
Young man:	Hey, what does that have to do with sex?
Marvin:	Absolutely everything, my friend. I promise. Do you want to hear the rest?
Young man:	Sure!
Marvin:	You pray always. With God's guidance you meet the woman He has picked out for you. You court her. You make certain that you have similar values. You pray together often. You both agree to make your marriage a three-way partnership with God.

Young man:	I thought you were going to tell me how to have great sex.
Marvin:	I'm almost to that part. Now, pay close attention. When you are certain you have found the girl God wants you to marry, you marry her before God. Then you add the ingredients that make sex the greatest thing either of you imagined.
Young man:	What ingredients?
Marvin:	Respect, commitment, and abundant love.That my young friend is the secret of a lasting love, a love that will blow your mind and bring you pleasure as long as you both shall live.

The above conversation never occurred. But if it had, and it was an honest conversation, the next question from the young man might be something like,

"Why can't sex be just as great and exciting with someone I just met? Why can't casual sex be just as exciting as that committed, 'save it for marriage' sex you described?"

If I didn't hear that question from a young man who had been exposed to a lot of TV and Movies and the Political Correctness of uncommitted sex, I would be surprised.

Just before the French, Existentialist philosopher Emile Camus died, he said that one of his greatest regrets was that he didn't have enough "recreational sex" during his lifetime. Recreational sex! That probably sounds great to a lot of Politically-Correct non-thinkers. Recreational sex sounds like something people do just for fun, with no consequences. That is the core of the PCL, that sex is nothing more than great fun, sport, a stress-reduction technique.

The Entertainment Industry works hard to promote the recreational sex concept. In the May 18 edition of Citizen Magazine, Paul Hess wrote in *They Call This Abstinence,* ". . . on television every year, there are over 20,000 acts of implied intercourse. This season, almost every middle adolescent (character) in television lost his or her virginity." The TV sex parade is constant. Doogie Howser goes skinny-dipping with a teacher. (We still call that sexual molestation of a minor where I come from.) Other soap-opera kids discover the wonder of homosexual sex. As far as I know, not a single one of those kids got pregnant, contracted an STD, such as AIDS and died a slow and painful death.

Origins Of Sexual Non-Think

In the '60s many people accepted the creed of "If it feels good, do it." "Establishment" was the ultimate dirty word. For the Politically Correct of the '60s establishment included traditions and institutions as basic as the family, marriage, and parenthood, and anything that smacked of doing what your parents did.

By the early '70s many had adopted a pseudo-intellectual position that anything that attacked the establishment was brilliant. The flower children shed their clothes, quit their jobs, and lit up their joints while heading to communes to demonstrate and share their brilliance with other brilliant dropouts.

One of the most heavily-targeted facets of the establishment was sex. It was, after all, sex that the fathers of the flower children had used to enslave their mothers.

In 1972, Phyllis Chesler wrote *Women and Madness.* In the book she informed us that the only strategy available to American women in defeating sexual oppression is "Sexual Suicide." She then illustrated her thesis by suggesting that the Nazis' use of slaves for industrial work was similar to the "prostitution" of female bodies by men. This book won front page placement and rave reviews from the New York Times Book Review.

Another jewel, singled out for recognition by the Times, was *Shappho was a Right-On Woman: A Liberated View of Lesbianism* by Sidney Abbott and Barbara Love. The Times, while lauding Lesbianism, condemned the family, calling it: *The Nuclear Family, That Cradle Of Evil.*

The Times' bashing of the family, while it championed Lesbianism as a creative and ingenious form of relationship, is illustrative of exactly what was wrong about the sexual revolution from its very beginning. The sexual perversion evangelists couldn't glorify their ideas about creative perversion, (or should we call their attempts at societal engineering right-brain deviancy) without bashing God, Religion, and Families. If sexual rodeos were such wonderful liberating events, why did they need to bash marriage and love and all of the things that God intended for inclusion in the package He calls Marriage? The pro-perversion crowd needed to bash families, along with the Omnipotent Family Designer, because in their heart of hearts they knew they were doing something very wrong. They didn't need to have memorized the biblical verses that instruct men and women on how to love each other. They already knew. It was in their genes. They knew they were wrong, as surely as Adam and Eve knew when it was time to don the fig leaves. Review the literature of the '70s and you will find that everyone who was pro-perversion was anti-God and anti-family. It felt good, writing this paragraph. I just wanted you to keep focused on not only what those folks were selling, but on what they were bashing.

In 1972, George and Nena O'Neil wrote *Open Marriage: A New Lifestyle For Couples.* The O'Neils suggested that a couple could expand their horizons by sexual encounters outside of the marriage. Predictably, they bashed traditional marriage with words like, " . . . archaic, rigid, outmoded, oppressive, static, decaying, Victorian . . . ."

The O'Neils never actually said that they thought marriage would or could be better with extramarital sexual liaisons. What they did was far more seductive. They suggested that the only people capable of handling these kinds of affairs were people whose "personhood" had not been overshadowed by the tyrannical dictates of "couplehood." You know the kind of folks the O'Neils were describing, those synergistic, open, growing in each other's presence, honest, open, creative, tolerant, people who could enjoy the liberation of open marriages.

In the contrived dialogue I used to begin this chapter I wasn't describing relationships according to Marvin, but relationships according to God. Marriage is a divine institution. It was not a coincidence that Christ performed his first miracle at a wedding.

It was, after all, through marriages that most of the flower children were admitted to the planet. You have to appreciate the power that Political Correctness had over America in the early '70s to understand why so many people took ideas like those espoused by the O'Neils, and used those ideas, to disrupt or ruin their relationships.

In his book *Sexual Suicide,* George Guilder points out that the O'Neils didn't seem to know the difference between equality and sameness. They observed that sex roles were limiting in behavior, and their solution was to level out the roles through an equal distribution of behavior. They suggested that if the husband made more money than the wife, then the wife should make more money. They also observed that since the roles (This is the O'Neil's perception of the roles.) of men were to fool around, then the woman should also fool around. This unreasonable reasoning merely illustrates the intellectual laziness of these liberal non-thinkers. In keeping with the spiritual bankruptcy of the times, the O'Neils never considered that philandering might be "Wrong." (That would have constituted establishment thinking.) They accepted the animal behavior in man (fooling around), and instead of attempting to rehabilitate men, they suggest women drop to the lowest common denominator and become promiscuous.

Defining Deviancy Down

I played High School football at John Carroll High in Birmingham, Alabama. Each year we played Childersburg High. The players from Childersburg must have had some sort of hormonal imbalance. Most of their players had fourteen inch necks on each side. They were very big, and very tough. They always managed to beat us senseless. The beatings from the Childersburg team was even worse when we played in their home town. Their football field was close to and downwind from a paper mill.

Now, everyone from the South who has ever been downwind from a paper mill probably knows what I am about to write. Paper mills make gigantic dairy farms smell like your favorite air freshener. They are putrid to the tenth power. When we played in Childersburg our coach couldn't figure out whether to bring us a few hours early so we could get accustomed to the stench, or to show up at the last minute so we weren't sick before the game got started.

Later in life, when I met people from Childersburg (who weren't trying to beat me senseless), they told me an amazing thing. They said that after a very short time, they got used to the smell. They got so used to the smell they never even noticed it. The Childersburgers prove my point as well as anyone could. You can get used to anything. You can, in fact, learn to take anything totally for granted.

As the perversion of the '70s became more and more widespread, we heard more and more about perversion. Perverts became the running stock of TV talk shows. Nudity and partial-nudity in movies went from something you could only see in "stag" films to something casual enough for people like Julie Andrews to try.

As perversion became increasingly commonplace, we as a nation began to define deviancy down. Here is an example of how we have defined deviancy down. In the '50s sodomy was recognized as a heinous act. It was carried on the books of many states as a felony. Something you have probably never heard a public figure say is that if we could stamp out sodomy we could do more to halt the spread of AIDS than all of the free condoms in the world will ever do. You won't hear that because sodomy has been defined down, way down, as deviant behavior. The fact is that if you were to publicly speak out against sodomy you would be condemned as a hateful, insensitive homophobic. The people behind the move to define sodomy down as deviancy are the people with the most at stake, the Sodomizers. The act of sodomy hasn't changed a bit, but its meaning has gone through a transition. In the past twenty years, the meaning of sodomy has gone from a very sick and perverted behavior, to a sacred subject of the *Politically Correct*.

Here is another example citizens over twenty years-old have witnessed. Not long ago the word "but" never had two T's. If I had said the B word with two T's my Mom would have immediately abandoned a family tradition. She would not have waited for my dad to come home to escort me to the garage. I would have caught a dose of corporal punishment on the spot. Today, everyone and anyone talks about kicking B___. Yes! I still spell it out. My parents are both in heaven, and I do not want one of my first chores in heaven to be explaining to Mom and Dad why I put that word in my book. It has been defined-down for most, but the young don't even know that once utterance of the B___ word was a dead give-away for a jerk. Today Beavis And B___head is the top-rated program on MTV. Most people would say, "so what?" or "it doesn't matter." I contend that each time we define deviancy down we lose part of who we are. The deviancy might be as seemingly harmless as the words we use, or as serious as the often life-threatening abandonment of sexual taboos. By defining deviancy down we lose much more than the boundaries that have defined our society. We lose part of *ourselves*.

Sexual Short Circuitry

You can take your pick of the theories about what attracts men and women to each other. D.H. Lawrence offered the unique idea that men select women for mates based on the woman's value in gaining the esteem of other men. One of the more popular theories is that men and women are attracted to each other based on their perception of reproductive powers. Men seek women who appear more capable for child-bearing and nursing. Women, according to the same theory, often seek out the more successful businessmen who represent the best "providers" of the tribe.

Whatever the magnet that attracts men to women is,it is predicated by our ultimate sex organ, the *brain*. We are either attracted to or repulsed by whatever our brains have decided is most appealing to us. Our brains are more complex than the world's most sophisticated computers. If man were to develop the ultimate computer, it would reach a point of development where it could grow no further without great technological developments in air-conditioning. We have come so far in the development of so called artificial intelligence that the inability to cool the machine would be the first hurdle we would meet if we did attempt to build the ultimate computer. If that ultimate computer did exist, it would still be one million times less capable of storing data than the human brain. Some people say we use only ten percent of our mental capacity. More learned scientists know that we don't even approach using ten percent of our brain.

Information is fed to the brain through the five senses. The brain interprets all of that information and we use the brain to make decisions.

Based on a combination of two things, we interpret the information collected through the five senses and processed by the brain. Then we *decide* what and how we will respond to various sexual stimuli. These two elements are:

1. The response elicited by the various stimuli. (If we smell a fragrance, see a certain color of hair, hear a particular kind of voice, taste a flavor on the lips of a lover, or feel a texture of skin, we are either turned on or turned off.)

2. Our predetermined understanding of what is right and wrong. (Acceptance of the "If it feels good, do it," philosophy eliminates this element from selecting responses to stimuli.)

Stimuli Are Linked. You can be thousands of miles from your lover and hear a song that you have heard while you were together. The song is linked to all of the pleasures you shared, and merely hearing the song triggers linkages in the brain to all of the pleasurable feelings you had together.

Because of the rapid fire operation of the brain in processing information from the five senses, all of our experiences, either pleasurable or painful, are linked together in packages. A replay of any one of these experiences has the ability to cause the brain to replay all of the feelings linked by the single experience to the entire event. So, simply hearing a love song brings back the package of feelings felt when holding your lover in front of a fireplace, while listening to *that* song, staring into her beautiful eyes, stroking her hair, enjoying the aroma of the burning apple wood, and possibly a hundred other stimuli all going off at once. Isn't God a good God to have given us such an immense capacity to enjoy love and life?

The problem of perversion comes when we receive stimuli that we know, because our values are wrong. We have the ability to either receive or reject those stimuli. The receptors in the brain are nothing more than receptors. They pick up whatever comes close to them. It is our human free will that we use to either accept and nourish what the brain receives, or to quickly expunge or reject information. The following are two stories of people who took no action to filter out what came into the brain, and acted on sick ideas.

Bubba's Sexuality

Bubba is 13 years-old. His body is involved in massive change. His voice is changing, and his body is beginning to sprout hair in some unexpected places as his physiology transitions from boyhood to manhood.

Probably the most dramatic of all of these changes is in Bubba's attitude. The awe he used to display when he played with his model cars has suddenly shifted to girls. Bubba is on the verge of one of life's greatest discoveries. Bubba is about to discover Bubbette.

If I made a list of all of the stimuli capable of igniting Bubba's volatile sexual engine this would be a very long book. Anything Bubba sees, smells, hears, tastes or feels could equate to a sexual signal as it careens through the caverns of his developing brain.

What do you imagine would happen to Bubba if, at about this time in his life, when his sexual development is in overdrive, he begins to receive some really warped stimuli? What if Bubba began to spend his weekends watching slasher movies? I'm talking about the ones with Sally Anne in the shower when weird Eddie comes creeping in and plants an axe in her head. Whoaaa! Bubba's brain is suddenly putting the wrong things into the same "turn on" file drawer. Bubba has now filed pretty young woman in the shower, with axe murder.

Does this sound bizarre? It is, and it is happening all over this country every night, in living rooms of parents who should know better. Bubba has access to every imaginable perverted scheme of sexuality available. Bubba's sexual development is very vulnerable to anything fed into his young skull. Bubba may or may not become a serial killer, but every time he mixes the stimuli of sex and violence he is *Learning*. Bubba's sexual beliefs and behavior will be a direct result of the things that he watches, hears, smells, tastes and feels. If Bubba is not learning restraint as he learns about his sexuality, then Bubba's sexual development is out of control.

A more troubling case is the story of Angelo. The first time Angelo can remember being turned on sexually, was using his father's pornography when he was ten. Angelo's dad had a collection of Child Pornography books, and because they were his father's books, Angelo had little trouble in accepting the concept that the things in the books were "Okay."

When Angelo was 12, he was babysitting for a six-year-old boy. He knew from the books what sex was all about, and he raped the boy. The development of Angelo's pedophilia was speeded along by societal acceptance (his Father's pornography).

In his late teens Angelo became associated with the North American Man Boy Love Association, (NAMBLA). They taught him that molesting young boys was a natural and "Okay" behavior.

Regardless of how sick the sexual perversion might be, there is someone, somewhere, or a group of people who will help convince you that whatever you want to do is a dandy idea.

Its estimated that there are 500 serial killers loose in America Today. Most or all of these murderers are operating off of very high-powered sex drives. These sex drives have been developed and encouraged by a society that is losing its values and subsequently all of its behavioral boundaries. A society where everything goes is a spawning ground for the sexually short-circuited. Instead of helping people to "re-wire" sick sex drives, America has become a virtual school for people who act out sick drives with pedophilia, bestiality, arson (long recognized as a sex-crime), rape, etc.

The Degeneracy of the Degenerators

I would not have included the following paragraphs in this book if I hadn't been inspired by a writer who displayed more courage than I, in his treatment of this subject. This confession, I hope, will illustrate all of our vulnerability to *Political Correctness*. Here I am, in a room surrounded by stacks of documentation, exposing the Politically Correct as whopper-mongers. On some recent days I have spent all my waking hours studying the intricacies of deceit used by the perpetrators of the Politically Correct lies. I am, in fact, a self-educated expert on Political Correctness. That does not mean that even I, an expert, can't become a victim. For months I have had an idea that I refused to communicate. The idea just seemed too silly to write about, too trivial, too unsubstantiated, too whimsical, too Politically Incorrect.

The idea that I resisted for so long was that the intellectual "experts" who wrote all of the sexual manifestos on the relevancy and, more often, the irrelevancy of morality in defining our sexuality, were often themselves sexual perverts. I had a strong feeling, a hunch, that the men and women who wrote sexual liberation declarations were themselves "sick sexual puppies."

The validation of my hunch and yet another reminder to trust my feelings on Political Correctness came from a book in the November 1993 issue of the *American Spectator*. The reviewer, George Jim Johnston, wrote about the book, *Degenerate Modems: Modernity as Rationalized Sexual Misbehavior* by E. Michael Jones.

In the book, Jones debunks theories that the perceived great modernist thinkers wrote in a sort of mentally detached state, not influenced by their own hangups. He wrote:

" . . . the crucial intellectual event occurs . . . when vices are transmitted into theories, when the 'intellectual' set-up-shop in rebellion against moral law and therefore against truth. All modern 'isms' follow as a result of this rebellion . . . . All of them can best be understood in the light of the moral disorders of their founders, proponents, and adherents."

Christians and most Conservatives have a set of rules we all use to govern our sexual behavior. We aren't turned off by words like "Govern" and we search for and embrace words despised by liberals, words like "right and wrong." *Degenerate moderns* begins with a literary home run on the importance of truth in determining behavioral standards. Jones quoted German Philosopher Josef Pieper who wrote:

"Since we nowadays think that all a man needs for the acquisition of truth is to exert his brain more or less vigorously, and since we consider an ascetic approach to knowledge hardly sensible, we have lost the awareness of the close bond that links the knowledge of truth to the condition of purity. Thomas Aquinas says that unchastity's first born daughter is blindness of spirit. Only he who wants nothing for himself, who is not subjectively 'interested' can know the truth. On the other hand, a selfishly corrupt will to pleasure destroys both resoluteness of spirit and the ability of the psyche to listen in silent attention to the language of reality."

Author Jones takes some of the work done by the champions of "If it feels good, do it" sexuality, and exposes their work as fraudulent attempts to justify their own deviancy.

Jones begins with a survey of the life and writings of Margaret Mead. The book, *Coming of Age In Somoa*, by Mead, is a blatant attempt to sell the "anything goes" version of sexual behavior as a panacea for mental health. Mead wrote lines like, " . . . lovers slip home from trysts beneath the palm trees or in the shadows of beached canoes," and her heros, " . . . laugh at stories of romantic love, scoff at fidelity and, as you might have guessed, smile on casual homosexual practices."

Mead's work was lauded (probably by fellow degenerates) as sexually liberating. People like Bertrand Russell used Mead's work as proof that as reviewer Johnston wrote, " . . . the sexual strictures of Judeo-Christianity were cultural accidents and that people could get along fine without them." It was the real scientists, like anthropologist Derek Freeman who exposed Mead's work as a blatant fraud. He reported that the Samoans were much more puritanical than Westerners, that they held female virginity in much higher esteem than Westerners, that they had and still have one of the highest rates of forcible rape in the world, and that they have a very high rate of suicides related to what Freeman called, "shame at illicit sexual unions." Jones said that Mead's report on Samoa was "about as scientific as the screenplay for the Blue Lagoon."

Mead's agenda certainly benefitted from her slant on the love life of the Samoans. While in Samoa, Mead, a married woman, was conducting two affairs—one with a man, and the other with her lesbian lover, fellow anthropologist Ruth Benedict. Mead considered herself a sexually-liberated New York Liberal. One of her ex-husbands probably said it best in a letter to Mead, when he said that her scientific reporting was in fact a, "dishonest way of treating your private affairs."

Jones doesn't miss an opportunity to write about the man who many think of simply as "The Great Man" or the "Father of Psychology." Freud was a sexually sick man, and he (using one of his sacred words) "projected" his sickness onto the world. Tragically, much of the world bought it. Jones suggested that the Oedipus complex is, "nothing more than Freud's personal history, and writ large. " Jones likens Freud's pronouncements on human sexuality to Bonnie and Clyde pontificating on the universal compulsion of humankind to rob banks.

Degenerate Moderns presents strong evidence that the evangelists for degeneracy are, very probably, degenerates themselves. An understanding of Jones' work makes it clearly relevant to ask questions about the authors of any "studies" of sexuality. We have recently been told that "studies" about the genetic predisposition of men to homosexuality were both objective and scientific. When we point out that most of the inconclusive studies were done by homosexuals, and ask if the sexual behavior of the scientists influenced their work, we are quickly told to shut up and stick to what is relevant. When we point out that Masters and Johnson are now divorced we are told that also is irrelevant. Believe this readers, it is relevant that many of the "experts" of the sexual revolution are writing about something they never had, sexual happiness. Keep asking those questions. They most certainly are relevant.

How Bad Is Bad?

One caller to my Radio Program called me a "Fuddy-Duddy." Another accused me of being "hyper-vigilant." Maybe I am just reacting to the sexuality of the "'90s." Maybe I am forgetting that men and women since Adam and Eve have dealt with sexual misbehavior. I write these pages because I think our sexual behavior has galloped out of control, and far beyond any reasonable bounds. Read the following paragraphs, and decide for yourself.

Snuff films were made and marketed for big bucks in the early 1980s. The movies featured standard pornographic sexual vignettes, but they were called snuff films because one or more of the "Stars" was killed, on camera, in the end of the movie. The victims, usually females, didn't suspect the very final endings of the movies. The consumers of the Snuff Films wanted to see those looks of terror on the faces of the victims just before they were killed.

Hospital Emergency Rooms are often the places where the depths of sexual perversion are exposed. One emergency room worker told me of having seen a six month old die from the effects of repeated rape and sodomy. In the Dallas Metroplex a seven-year-old girl had to have part of a ratchet wrench surgically removed. She had been raped repeatedly by her 30-year-old father, and his 61 year-old father. The girl reportedly was forced to look at pornographic magazines depicting a woman performing sexual acts on herself with tools and then act out what she had seen. Balch Springs Detective Gary Moore, who investigated the ratchet wrench case said, "There are some sick, sick, sick people in this world."

TV Talk Shows consistently provide forums for the "sick, sick, sick people," and in so doing, they grant them the *Politically Correct* Seal of Approval. Larry King interviewed the President of NAMBLA, the North American Man-Boy Love Association. Donahue did a show featuring a 38-year-old woman living in a conjugal relationship with a 14-year-old boy.

Sex For Sale is the title of a special report on world-wide prostitution, in the July 21, 1993 issue of Time magazine. The report describes the way the Korean-controlled nude modeling studios in Houston, Texas are supplied with prostitutes. American GIs in Korea are given $5,000 to marry Korean Girls. When they return to Fort Hood, Texas, they receive another $5,000 to divorce the girls, and turn them over to their Houston pimps. The "Human Cargo" flows two ways, with Los Angeles girls being conned into signing contracts to sing, dance and entertain in the Orient. When the American girls arrive in Asia they are forced into prostitution.

Child Prostitution is a huge business in America. I will never forget a conversation with a social worker who had worked for years with incarcerated children. She had been talking to a 15-year-old girl who was returning to her home in a large American city. The Social Worker asked, "You aren't going back out on the streets again, are you?" The girl replied, "I couldn't make much money if I wanted to. Men want young girls. Its hard to make a living on the streets if you are over 13."

U.S. Prostitutes Under the Age of 18 number from between 90,000 to 300,000. Many pedophiles are practicing their deviancy during foreign "Sex Tours," that exploit children, especially children in Asia. According to a Time magazine report, dozens of travel agencies cater to this clientele. A guide to the world's sex spas for homosexuals seeking young boys called Spartacus International Gay Guide, is published in Germany in several languages. In August of '93, Lauda Airlines, an Austrian-based airline owned by former auto racing champ Niki Lauda, promoted child sex tourism in its in-flight magazine.

Middle School Children in a San Marcus, California school began turning up pregnant in record numbers. An investigation revealed that after school the kids went to a student's home where they viewed his father's pornographic videos, and then acted out what they saw.

These paragraphs have been harsh. Most indictments are. This entire chapter is a tocsin to those who cling to the belief that our kids are just doing the '90s version of what our parents did. These few paragraphs are a summary of how far into the septic tank of immorality our nation has gone. Whenever a nation abdicates the function of the brain to the genitals, that nation sinks to a level of behavior lower than the level of behavior normally ascribed to animals.

Animal Behavior

In 1991, New Mexico State University sponsored a public performance of a man from California who, while naked, preformed a one-man show on stage. On my radio program I objected to a State-Funded University using *my* tax money (I always personalize the use of tax money, and wish everyone else did the same) to pay this character to jump around on a stage naked. One young woman who described herself as an art student challenged me. I did an excellent job in my effort to stop laughing. (I am continuously amazed at some of the public acts of obscenity the liberals categorize as art.)

The young woman was sincere in her attempt to explain to me the error of my ways, and why the naked man was a performing artist. I thanked her, and listened. She said the man was simply trying to remind his audience that we were all animals. Admittedly, that was as long as I listened. I reminded her that some lions ate their young, and that I have never contemplated eating my children. I also told the caller that I resented being called an animal. I have an animal nature, but it is also part of my repertoire of living skills to be able to control my animal nature.

I could have been talking to my hub caps. Liberals either don't recognize, or meticulously avoid dealing with their spiritual nature on anything other than the most superficial level. Inadvertently, my caller had stumbled on the very core belief of the sexual revolution. The Liberals who made the sexual revolution happen, believe the beast in us reigns supreme. Since they have no linkage with God, they see no need or advantage in controlling their animal nature. "If it feels good do it," is not a joke. It is for people who have bought a creed for living from the sexual revolution.

If you accept the supremacy of man's animal nature you are ready to join the *Politically Correct* and embrace lies such as "Kids are going to do it (have sex) anyway."

The Sex Information and Education Council of The United States (SIECUS) publishes manuals for sex education. In *Sex, Science and Values* (Study Guide Number 9) February, 1969, by Harold T. Christiansen, we learn that:

"The strict Judeo-Christian code inherited from the past, in which chastity is prescribed, is being challenged. Rational inquiry is replacing blind faith . . . . This newer, relativistic position on sexual morality is a rational one backed up by research . . . this is the approach that seems to offer the most hope for consensus under modern conditions." (Translation: Forget God and all of His teachings. Follow Siecus. Chastity is a loser. Have sex, and be happy like animals.)

Man has an animal nature. It can be one of his best features, if it is mastered, and always kept subordinate to man's spiritual nature. Whenever man allows his animal nature to rule he becomes less than an animal.

The '80s, AIDS, and the Birth of America's Greatest Whopper Or: Quickly! Bring Some Gasoline to Put Out This Fire!

In the early '80s, America began to meet its newest unwanted neighbor, the AIDS virus. For a short while, we as a nation held our collective breath as we considered the potency of this poison.

Throughout history calamities have been turned into good things by a people willing to adapt. The South is punctuated with statues to the Boll Weevil, the bug that exterminated the cotton crop and motivated the South to devise other ways to make their livelihood.

For a very brief time the AIDS virus held the potential to be a Boll Weevil to America. We could have accepted the deadlines of the disease, admitted that the disease was spread by behavior, and done a massive behavioral overhaul to stop AIDS in its tracks. Many did, and still do, believe that would have been the only logical, or sane response to what everyone knew from the start—that AIDS could very quickly become a major epidemic. We missed our best chance of stopping AIDS.

Instead of moving to limit the behavior that causes AIDS, we moved to obscure the cause and cover up the reality of AIDS with the myth of Safe Sex. The Safe Sex Movement, the *Politically Correct* "solution" to the AIDS scourge has caused the exact opposite of what it was intended to do. AIDS is caused by sexual promiscuity. The Safe Sex Myth increased promiscuity. The following two quotes illuminate the profundity of the error we made in perpetrating the Safe Sex Myth.

In 1972, Professor Kingsly Davis, in a U.S. Government Report titled, *The American Family, Relation To Demographic Change*, wrote:

"The current belief that illegitimacy will be reduced if teenage girls are given an effective contraceptive is an extension of the same reasoning that created the problem in the first place. It reflects an unwillingness to face problems of social control and social discipline while trusting some technological device to extricate society from its difficulties. The irony is that the illegitimacy rise occurred precisely while contraceptive use was becoming more, rather than less, widespread and respectable."

William A. Donohue, the Chairman of the Department of Sociology at LaRoche College in Pittsburgh, wrote in a paper titled *Why We Have An Increase In Teenage Pregnancy,* published in the October, 1990 edition of The American Family Association Journal.

"If we had set out deliberately to create an environment likely to foster American adolescent's recklessness, we could hardly have done any better than to embrace the New Freedom. When society drops its guard everyone takes note, and none more attentively than young people. Conversely, when society raises its vigilance, none feels the difference more forcefully than the youth. Unfortunately, that has not happened.

Mapping Our Sexual Behavior

I present here an outline of the steps we took getting into this sexual morass of the '90s. The amazing thing about our national sexual problems is that they are still solvable. While simple and obvious solutions exist in the acceptance of behavioral responsibility and commitment to positive change, the powers that have chauffeured us into this mess adamantly cling to what they themselves have proven *Does not work.*

American Sexual Behavior–Downhill Flow

Sex On Day One—Man did not invent sex. Adam and Eve were born with the ability to participate in sexual activity, and to enjoy each other sexually. They had no sex manuals. They knew all they needed to know.

Thoughout history, observers of sexual behavior have categorized the sexuality of cultures as either:

A. Sexually Liberated (Leaning toward an absence of values and boundaries.)

B. Repressed (Based on values or boundaries.)

1962—Political Correctness Era began with Supreme Court Decisions taking God, Prayer, and Godly behavior out of Public Schools. Our nation, with those acts, turned its back on God, and almost immediately God began turning His back on us. The sexual revolution of the '60s was governed by a creed of "if it feels good do it." These years were also called the anti-establishment years, and included bashing God, Religion, Family, etc.

1972—The O'Neils' Open Marriage concept lent a pseudo-intellectual and Politically Correct blessing to extra martial promiscuity.

The '70s were a time of *Creative Perversion* or *Right Brain Degeneracy.* The open marriages led the way for the "Swingers," and Marriage Under God continued to be bashed.

The '80s began with the AIDS Horror. The Politically Correct fabricated the Safe Sex Myth to keep the sexual revolution alive.

Today organizations such as the NEA, Planned Parenthood, and the ACLU are, in effect, attempting to have school children taught how to be promiscuous.

The C Word (Revised Version)

These words are for my dear friend, Lu Lu. Mrs. Lu Lu is one of those wonderful ladies who carries enough spirituality with her to seem like a sort of Mother to everyone. Lu Lu frequently called a TV talk show I hosted in Alamogordo, New Mexico. One evening Lu Lu called and told me that she was really upset with me. Lu Lu wanted me to stop talking about *Condoms* on TV.

Both Lu Lu and I grew up in a different time, a time when we didn't talk publicly about condoms. If my Mom was still alive she probably would have been on the phone, with Lu Lu, setting me straight.

Ten, or even five years ago I wouldn't have talked publicly about condoms. It would have been bad manners. I often talk about condoms now because our kids hear so much about them from the people who are supposed to be leading them out of illiteracy. I talk about condoms because to Liberals the "C" word has become the great solution to all of America's sexual problems. I talk about condoms because they are the subject of a preposterous lie.

I suggest that we shelve those condoms that don't work anyway, and adopt a new "C" word, a "C" word guaranteed to solve the problems the condoms have been exacerbating. The other "C" word is Commitment. If we could return to the value that sex was something people saved for marriage, for the commitment of a lifetime, we could save the lives and preserve the integrity of our children. (We could also get Lu Lu to stop fussing at me.)

Abstinence Is Not a Myth

Abstinence is not some pipe dream of a old priest that people won't or can't use. The entertainment field is packed with examples of no consequence sex, and far too many young people take what they see demonstrated on General Hospital and use those farces to set their own behavioral standards. The truth is that there are plenty of sane role models youth could truly admire, for instance, men like A.C. Green.

A.C. Green is a six-foot nine-inch starter for the Los Angeles Lakers. He plays a sport filled with men who flaunt their sexual exploits like their rebounding records. Wilt Chamberlain wrote an autobiography boasting that he had bedded 20,000 women. A.C. Green is not some namby pamby follow-the-leader clown.

He sets his own standards, and one standard he has set for himself is sexual purity.

In an interview in the June 1993 issue of Dr. James Dobson's Focus On The Family magazine Mr. Green was quoted as having said, "I will take a stand for Christ. I'm proud to say that I am a virgin, and I don't hide the strength God has given me."

Shhh! Can't you hear it? It's the sound of a revival in this land of ours. A.C. Green is one of many men who are going to turn things around, and re-educate America about the strength in purity and the moral shallowness of promiscuity. Listen! Believe! Join the fight today!

There was a time when Lu Lu was exactly right, and condom was a dirty word. Now, thanks to the insidious growth of *Political Correctness*, Virginity and Abstinence have become our new dirty words. Its a lie. We all know it. Abstinence is for real men, and dynamic young women. Virginity is something that really tough guys and truly intelligent girls can maintain. This war is winnable, and the victory becomes more visible with every adult who commits to become a teacher and a leader, and with every youth who commits to God's plan of purity. There is more super-exciting news on the subject in the next chapter.

Chapter 7

The Safe Sex Myth

The Problem

- One baby in six is born to teenage parents.
- In New York City one baby in three is born to an unwed mother.
- Thirty-three thousand cases of Sexually Transmitted Diseases (STDs) are transmitted daily, about fourteen million per year.
- One million six hundred thousand abortions occur annually.
- The teenage abortion rate has doubled since 1968.

Causes of the Problem

The Alan Guttmacher Institute is the research arm of Planned Parenthood, or as I refer to these people, Banned Parenthood or Planned Barrenhood. The Guttmacher Institute, in a paper by Elsie Jones et al., titled *Teenage Parenthood In Developed Countries: Determinents And Policy Implications,* Published in Family Planning Perspectives, Volume 17, March/April 1985, identified these four factors for the teenage pregnancy problem.

  1. Inadequate sex education material.
  2. Inept use of contraceptives by American teenagers.
  3. Ineffective health services.
  4. "Reactionary" pressures from Christian groups.

I don't believe the Alan Guttmacher folks even came close to identifying the causes of the problem. Here is what I believe are much more accurate *Causes* of the teenage pregnancy problems.

1. The refusal of Planned Parenthood to acknowledge the truth of reports funded by themselves (The Guttmacher Institute) and their dogged determination for teaching that sexual behavior is "acceptable" if condoms are used.

2. Obliviousness to all of the studies (from the AMA and the FDA) that prove conclusively that condoms exacerbate the problems they are supposed to solve.

3. The work of the cabal of Planned Parenthood, The National Education Association (NEA), the Sex Information and Education Council of The United States (SEICUS) and of the ACLU to prohibit the use of abstinence-based programs that do solve teenage pregnancy problems.

4. The prevailing national obsession of this nation with sex, and the media's monetary stake in promoting the lie that all sex is okay if condoms are used.

I don't even have a Ph.D. and I surely don't head a research institute, but believe I did a lot better job of identifying the causes of the problem than the Guttmacher Institute did. You decide.

No Parents Allowed

The NEA passed a resolution calling for "Privileged Communications" between teachers and students. That sounds okay, doesn't it? Shouldn't teachers and children be able to talk privately, free from worry about what someone else might think of their conversation? Don't be too hasty with your answer.

Children at a high school in Las Cruces, New Mexico were given a brief form from the school-based clinic. They could check off whether or not they wanted their parents to be excluded from any "counseling" they had at the clinic.

Is this the same Public Education System that as recently as five years ago would not issue a Band-Aid or an Aspirin to a student without parental permission? Sure is. The difference is that this sex education is something that, according to the sex educators, parents don't seem to be able to handle. If parents are cut out of the loop, then kids can pick up their condoms, get advice on exactly how to have sex (heterosexual or homosexual), and if the need arises, have abortions without their parents ever knowing about it.

A public-service announcement from Planned Parenthood begins by asking if there are things that you can't talk to your parents about? In a soothing tone, the announcer suggests that those wonderful folks at Planned Parenthood really care, and that they will be discreet. They pull up just a hair short of saying, "Hey, we know you want to hide things from your parents, and we'll help you do exactly that."

Mrs. Millie Pogna, who serves on the New Mexico State Board of Education, sent a letter to parents of school children, warning them of an attempt to exclude parents from the knowledge of what sex education tactics were being used in public schools. She began her letter by telling parents when and where an HIV/AIDS workshop was being held. Mrs. Pogna wrote, "If at all possible, please try and attend this workshop. They may well try to prohibit 'outsiders' (parents) from attending, but just tell them that I suggested you attend . . . ."

There is a nationwide conspiracy to keep parents out of the public schools. In the past, parents never needed people like Mrs. Pogna to pressure school boards concerning unannounced meetings, restricted workshops, or school-based clinics that give students the suggestion to eliminate their parents from "certain" discussions with teachers who want to mold their children without the intrusion of parents.

Why all the secrets? What in the world is going on in schools that they don't want us to know about? I'll give you a clue, and it sounds like sex education.

Some Call it Sex Education

I warn you now. I am going to use material being taught in some of America's Public Schools. This is rough stuff. When I began broadcasting, I worked at a small AM Station. Located down the hall was an FM Rock and Roll Station. One day I talked on the radio about a sex education curriculum being used for sixth graders. The curriculum included detailed information about how to preform Anilingus. I said that anyone who would suggest such a depraved activity to kids had to be a very sick person. I also said that anyone who told sixth graders that this activity, which even wel-bread dogs avoid, was "acceptable" had no business being employed in a public school. After my show one of the DJ's from the FM Station asked, "How do you get away with saying things like that on the air?" This was a legitimate question from a man who plays Guns and Roses and Madonna music. Remember, I was merely talking about what is **Actually being taught to sixth graders**.

In the past, *Boys and Sex* and *Girls and Sex,* two books by Wardell Pomeroy, Ph.D., a co-author of the *Kinsey Reports*, was recommended reading for sixth graders in Milwaukee, and elsewhere. Here are some suggestions Dr. Pomeroy passes on to sixth graders from *Boys and Sex:*

"I have known cases of farm boys who had a loving sexual relationship with an animal and who felt good about their behavior until they got to college where they learned for the first time that what they had done was 'abnormal.' Then they were upset . . . ."

Authors Note: In case you missed that one readers, the writer is saying that bestiality is normal. If this genius were a college dorm director would he have some rooms equipped with stables? As you read some of these gems think of a decent sixth grader listening to this drivel coming from a respected teacher.

More from Dr. Pomeroy:

"Premarital intercourse does have its definite values as a training ground for marriage or some other committed relationship . . . ."

Can you imagine sixth grade Jasper calling Wanda Sue and saying, "If your folks are going to be out this evening, I'd like to come over and use you and your bedroom as a training ground in case I ever get into a marriage or other committed relationship?" I don't know what kind of school you went to but there were girls in my sixth grade class who would have told their dads if I had said something like that, and I would have been "instant" history.

I just read Rush Limbaugh's new book *See I Told You So*, and he made an appropriate decision to eliminate this kind of material from his book. He assured his readers that he could provide some really sickening stuff, but he didn't. I choose to give you samples of this bilge because I am determined to have you appreciate our current dilemma. Besides, Rush's book is primarily for entertainment. This book is intended to be a text on how to recognize and defeat Political Correctness. As you continue to read, keep reminding yourself that this is what has been taught to small children.

Still more from Dr. Pomeroy, " Boys and girls who start having intercourse when they're adolescents, expecting to get married later on, will find that it's a big help in finding out whether they are really congenial or not; to make everyday-life comparisons, it's like taking a car out for a test run before you buy it."

Again, think of the sixth graders. They are listening to this guy, and thinking, "I wonder what congenial means. It must mean . . . ." What does congenial mean? Again, think of Jasper calling Wanda, and asking, "Want to go out for a test run?"

More from Pomeroy, in *Girls and Sex*, "Sex play with boys (or, for that matter, with girls) can be exciting, pleasurable, and even worthwhile in the sense that it will help later sexual adjustment."

Let's take a spot check. How many of you dads would appreciate having Conroy talk this way to your daughter in a co-ed class? I know that many Liberals wouldn't tolerate it, but that is a moot point since they usually send their kids to private schools.

Here is a sample of the wisdom from the widely-used text by John J. Burt and Linda Bower Meeks, *Education For Sexuality, Concepts And Programs For Teaching*,

"How does one intelligently decide among these alternatives:

permissiveness	vs.	commitment
premarital chastity	vs.	premarital sex
heterosexuality	vs.	homosexuality
marital fidelity	vs.	promiscuity

"Discussion and research into this variety of behaviors have led us to the conclusion that no single alternative or set of alternatives holds a monopoly on happiness. Hence, alternatives must be decided on an individual basis. There are no common absolutes."

In the same book, the authors provide six questions children should ask themselves to determine if they are ready for sex. As you read these questions, recall what sexual arousal felt like and how it influenced you when you were 12 or 13 years old. Think about a sexually excited 13-year-old, rushing back to his book to check and see if he was ready for sex.

1. "Am I trying it to prove something to others? To myself? How do I really feel about having sex right now? How does my partner feel?"
2. "What feelings do I have for the other person?"
3. "Do we communicate well?"
4. "Do I have accurate information about sex?"

5. "Are we willing to take full responsibilities for
   our actions?"
6. "Are we loving, caring friends?"

If you don't see the total inappropriateness of such a list for children, and if you don't recognize anyone who would suggest such a list for children as deranged, I don't believe you remember what it felt like to be sexually aroused when you were 13 years-old.

Homosexual Deceit

The sex-ed curriculums being forced on America's youth teach that homosexuality is "different," an alternative lifestyle. In *Changing Bodies, Changing Lives: A Book For Teens On Sex And Relationships*, Random House, 1980, we can learn that:

"Fear and prejudice go away quickest when you can meet some open homosexuals and know them . . . .The rest of this is maybe a way for you to 'meet' some gay and lesbian teenagers indirectly . . . ."

None of the liberal sex-education material bothers to inform youth that homosexuals are at a very high risk for AIDS, or that suicide is the leading cause of death among homosexuals. The truth is, there is very little that is actually "gay" about being a homosexual.

In New York, an attempt was made to introduce the *Children of the Rainbow* curriculum into elementary schools. The curriculum featured such homosexual propaganda as *Heather Has Two Mommies, Gloria Goes To Gay Pride,* and *Daddy's Roommate*. The *Children of the Rainbow Curriculum*, along with New York City Superintendent of Schools, Joseph Fernandez were thrown out together when parents demanded that the foolishness stop in their schools.

In other schools where homosexuality is taught as an "alternative," there has been a predictable confusion among teenagers. Being a teenager is tough enough without someone promoting homosexuality in our schools. In July, 1993, the Washington Post ran an article on how students were "questioning their sexuality" now that homosexuality had become "cool." The Post suggested the confusion had been predicated by "publicity about the gay-rights movement and lessons learned in sex-education classes."

The arrival of sexual confusion, as a result of homosexual promotion in public schools, has produced a negative effect. Sex-education classes have consistently fueled the problems they were designed to solve. In other words, sex education about homosexuality is not helping anyone. Ironically, that is consistent with education in our public schools.

Stressing Abstinence

The educational regulations for the state of New Mexico direct educators to "stress abstinence" in sex education programs. That wording was obviously too ambiguous to stop State Superintendent of Schools, Allen Morgan, from participating in an Albuquerque High School Safe Sex High School Assembly.

The Assembly featured two experts on AIDS Transmission. They were experts because they were HIV-Positive. We can appreciate the fact that people are trying to do something to prevent the spread of AIDS, and it would seem that people with the disease know more about it than people who haven't contracted it. Not necessarily! I'm an alcoholic, and I am often asked to speak on the subject. My expert status didn't occur during my twenty-five years of drinking. I became an expert when I learned enough about being an alcoholic to stop drinking the stuff. I drank for twenty-five years, but my expertise is based on six years of sobriety. The same reasoning applies to people with AIDS. They aren't experts until they really understand how they got the disease and how to prevent it. Consider what the experts told the children at the assembly in Albuquerque, and you decide if they are qualified experts.

The presenters were male and female. The man, a bald fellow who called himself "Bald Paul," told the kids that they needed to use condoms. He said, "anytime you guys get into inclement weather, wear your raincoat. And you ladies have got every right to demand the wet-weather gear."

In a few pages, I'll arm you with devastating facts on the utter stupidity of condom use. For now, I ask you to believe that telling children to use condoms when they have sex is an industrial-strength "no-brainer."

Don't misunderstand me. An AIDS victim could have a tremendous impact talking to children. However, the effectiveness of the message is dependent on the genuine sincerity of the speaker. If an AIDS victim delivered a message (the true message) of, "I thought I was immortal and did it anyway. But no condom in the world can keep you from dying." That would help tremendously— simply because it is the truth.

The lie continues, from Bald Paul's telling the "whooper" in Albuquerque to Magic Johnson's telling it in print. Contrary to what anyone may choose to believe, it doesn't matter how many people tell a lie. IT is still a lie.

The assembly in Albuquerque sounded more like a pep rally for latex than an intelligent presentation of truth. It didn't come close to the spirit of the New Mexico Staff Educational Regulation directing that abstinence be stressed. The person who arranged the assembly probably could counter my accusation with something as lame as, "Well, we talked about abstinence at another time and place." To appreciate the fallacy of vaguely-worded directions such as "abstinence shall be stressed" recall again the nature of the audience.

Consider a vignette from the lives of two Albuquerque, New Mexico High School Students—Bubba, and his date for the evening, Bubbette. The scene opens in a dark parking lot, where we find the couple in the front seat of Bubba's father's pickup truck.

"Ohhhhh, Bubbette! You drive me crazy," says Bubba, blowing a blast of onion breath into Bubbette's ear.

If this were a movie, *Johnny Comes Marching Home Again* would be playing in the background.

"Slow down, Bubba."

"Why, darlin. You know I'm crazy about you, and I'm gonna let you wear my letter jacket till Wednesday."

As Bubba talks he quickly applies a hammer lock to his opponent, eh!, date.

"Bubba, I'm not ready for this."

The music changes now, going to the theme from *Bonanza*. There is a pause before Bubba delivers the line that shines the light of truth on his educational accomplishments.

"But Darlin, they said in Sex-Education class that if we really loved each other we could use a condom."

Stop the Movie

Before we continue, let's think about what actually happened in Bubba's Sex-Education class. He sat in that classroom and listened, more or less attentively, for fifty-five hours of film, discussion, lecture and demonstration. Abstinence was stressed. Actually only about fifteen minutes were spent discussing the use of condoms. To appreciate Bubba's learning we must understand how learning occurs. We tend to filter out what we don't much care about, and to heavily emphasize what we want to hear, or learn. If all that had been said during the entire fifty-five hours, about condoms, had been these words. "If you are going to do it anyway, be sure to use a condom." what would Bubba have heard? Bubba would have summarized the entire course, all fifty-five hours, with the one sentence:

"If you are going to do it anyway, use a condom."

Will Bubba and Bubbette stake their future on the condom that has been in Bubba's wallet for fifteen months? Considering that they sat together in Sex Education class your guess is as good as mine. The fact is that these two children are about to make a very important decision that will affect them for the rest of their lives, and their decision will be based on what they have been taught, and they have been taught a lie.

Fantasy In Latex

There is nothing inherently evil about a condom. All a condom is, is a sheath of latex, that fails miserably at the job it was designed to do. The real tragedy of condoms is that they are being held up by the Liberals as a solution to America's Sexual problems.

Sex educators are, in effect, sending young troops into combat with faulty gear. Those educators would not do what they are telling our children to do.

In 1960, I attended U.S. Army Basic Training at Fort Jackson, South Carolina. I remember well a drill Sergeant standing in front of crowded bleachers teaching us how to use the M-1 Rifle.

The Sergeant said, "The recoil from this weapon will not hurt you."

Immediately my mind rejected what I had just heard. That rifle was too big, and made too much noise not to recoil like the kick of a healthy mule. As I was disbelieving what the instructor had just said, he made a believer out of me. He loaded the rifle, placed the butt directly into his crotch, and pulled the trigger. He then selected the most terrified member of our platoon and had the soldier repeat what he had just watched the Sergeant do. To this day I am a true believer that, if held snugly against yourself, the M-1 rifle recoil will not hurt you. That sergeant won my trust by demonstrating that he believed what he said enough to conduct an extraordinary demonstration.

Sex educators don't have the courage to practice what they are teaching our children. I don't believe any other incident illustrates the flakiness of sex educators as much as the following. To me, this event is proof positive that most sex educators are talking the talk, but wouldn't dare to walk the walk.

These are the words of Dr. Theresa Crenshaw, a former president of the American Association of Sex Education, Counselors, and Therapists:

"On June 19, 1987, I gave a lecture on AIDS to 800 sexologists at the World Conference of Sexology in Heidelberg. Most of them had recommended condoms to their clients and students. I asked that if they had the partner of their dreams, and knew that person carried the virus, would they have sex while depending on a condom for protection? No one raised their hand. After a long delay, one timid hand surfaced from the back of the room. I told them that it was irresponsible to give advice to others that they would not follow themselves. The point is, putting a mere balloon between a healthy body and a deadly disease is not safe."

What a cavalier attitude! Suggesting that human beings use condoms for avoidance of pregnancy and for protection from AIDS is like a jump master telling troopers that only eighteen percent of the parachutes don't open, so go ahead and count on your chute opening. This would never happen, because jump masters sometimes are required to jump with their troops. If there was some justice, and high schoolers could tell their sex education teachers, "You first, Teacher" we would see a quick end to the Safe Sex Myth.

Hey! Fun For All!

If there were academy awards for stupidity in sex education one should be reserved for the administrators at Chelmsford

High School in Chelmsford, Mass. On April 8, 1972, they brought in a special sex education program conducted by Suzi Landolphi, and her company, Hot, Sexy And Safer Productions, Inc. (It is relevant to point out that Ms. Landolphi owns several condom stores.)

The following are comments from Ms. Landolphi's presentation which was videotaped:

"I can't believe how many people came here to listen to somebody talk about sex, instead of staying home and having it yourself."

Author's note: The students were age 14 and older. "What we're gonna do is we're gonna have a group sexual experience here today. How's that? . . . . With audience participation . . . ."

"Hey I'll take your brother or your sister. It doesn't matter to me. I don't care . . . .You get less rejection that way."

Barbara Ward, chairperson of the Chelmsford School Committee saw the presentation, and said the performance was both entertaining and educational. Barbara probably lost the confidence of parents in Chelmsford who sued the School Committee, the Superintendent and other officials. The complaints alleged that Ms. Landolphi broke several laws by requiring sexual activity from children under 16.

Guess what Ms. Landolphi had to say? (Liberals would probably call this enlightenment), She said,

"I do a performance that is based on self-worth and self-confidence. I describe safer sex as honest and clear communication."

Higher Education

Safe sex education isn't just for the kids. Its also a part of "higher education." I hope you appreciate my description of this next display. It was paid for and sponsored by the school. You should appreciate it, you paid for it.

The University of California at Irvine used a "Safe Sex" display during "Health Week." The display, which was set up in the University's food court, included three signs. The first sign read *Safe*, and had the word abstinence on it. The second sign read *Safer*, along with the words, "Masturbation, fantasy, massage, kissing/licking with or without oral-genital contact, sex toys and talking." The last sign featured the words *Safest* and listed "vaginal or anal intercourse with condom, oral sex on male with condom, oral sex on female with dental dam, oral or anal sex with dental dam." There were, of course, free condoms for all. A student manning the table, invited students to demonstrate condom use on plastic models, while he danced around holding a plastic penis to his crotch.

Ventilated Condoms

The AMA said that condoms have an eighteen percent failure rate. Well, that didn't impress those folks at Planned Parenthood. They stuck to their story, and kept passing out condoms, including the red ones inside their valentines. (No fooling! They were supplying kids with condom-loaded valentines.) Then the Food and Drug Administration got into the act. In laboratory tests they found that condoms failed, close to a third of the time. They also cautioned people to remember that the laboratory tests had not included something the condoms would have to endure under actual field conditions, "Friction and Movement."

Now to the part about the ventilated condoms. The FDA revealed that the holes in the condoms were about 100 times larger than the AIDS virus. Imagine this—I'm six feet tall. Six feet times a hundred is 600 feet. That is exactly the size of two football fields, from goal line to goal line, laid out next to each other. Imagine a door six-hundred feet high and six-hundred feet wide. Do you reckon I could squeeze through that door?

Now, do you reckon an AIDS virus could slip through a hole one hundred times its own size?

In its continuing campaign of misinformation the CDC will remind you of a study in Europe where 123 healthy Europeans, using condoms, had sex for over a year with an infected partner, and not one of them contracted the disease. They left out the information about the gender of the infected partners. That is relevant because its much harder for a woman to infect a man than visa versa.

If someone quotes that study to you, tell them about the study reported on by Dr. Margaret Fischl in a 1987 issue of the *AMA Journal*. In that University of Miami study, where all of the husbands had AIDS, seventeen percent of the wives were HIV Positive after a year and a-half of condom-protected sex.

It was around the time that the FDA released their studies that Safe Sex became "Safer" sex. Believe me, I don't intend to nit-pick here, but if something isn't safe, we shouldn't call it "Safer." Less than safe is *Dangerous!* Calling sex, "Dangerous Sex" wouldn't do, because it violates the "tradition" of sex education in America!

Guess What Really Works

Bill Bennett said it so well, "Abstinence Works Every Time It's Used." Liberals will be quick to pounce on that one, and shout, "But kids are going to do it (have sex) anyway. You can't stop them." Liberals shout things like that because, going back to our earlier definitions, liberals themselves are "lacking in moral restraint." Liberal sex educators, whose libidos out-function their brains, simply can't think of students taking responsibility for their sexuality.

A study conducted by the U.S. Department of Health and Human Services, along with the State of Utah, and a similar two-year study of the effect of abstinence studies in Illinois examined the results of three Abstinence Programs. The programs

were *Teen Aid, Sex Respect*, and *Values And Choices*. For sta-
tistical data on those studies, and for more information on those
programs, I suggest that you try to obtain a copy of Family
Voice, the March 1993 issue, Volume 15, Number 3. (Write
Concerned Women For America at 370 L'Enfant Promenade,
S.W., Suite 800, Washington, D.C. 20024.)

I believe that one of the most dynamic endorsements for
Abstinence Education in American schools came from some of
the maintenance staff in San Marcos, California, Middle School.
After the program had been taught, the people who maintain
the school facilities reported that the students were showing
considerably more respect for themselves and for the facility.
The students were more courteous, and more respectful of
themselves, each other, and of their surrounding. Funny, don't
you think? With the "Left" going on campaigns to save the spot-
ted owl, perhaps one of the best ideas for environmental awareness comes from the "Right" in the form of Abstinence-Based
Sex Education.

Puzzle Solving 101

These are the facts:

- Sex Education Classes stressing condom distribution
  only create the need for more condoms, and supply a
  steady stream of customers for the Abortion Industry.
- Abstinence-based Education works.

If condoms don't work, but abstinence does, then what
would you imagine a logical national leader would give the
American children?

Forget logic. The Liberal agenda rules, and Mr. Bill appointed Joycelyn Elders, the High Priestess of Condom Distribution as his Surgeon General. This is the woman who
evangelizes what she calls, "The Condom Solution." This is the
woman who wants sex education to begin in Kindergarten. She

is a national cheerleader for abortion-on-demand, and she continuously recites her battle cry of "Planned and wanted" babies.

Dr. Elders said pro-life people should, "get over their love affair with the fetus." and "Love little babies as long as they are in somebody else's uterus," and "Look who's fighting the pro-life movement a—celibate, male-dominated church."

Remembering that this woman has immense power to shape our sex-education program as a nation, consider her words on that subject, "We taught teenagers what to do in the front seat of the car; now it's time to teach them what to do in the back seat."

Yes, this is the same Dr. Elders who refused to tell teenagers in Arkansas that she had accidently distributed defective condoms to them. When asked why she didn't go public with this blunder she announced, "I didn't want to hurt the program."

Today workers at the U.S. Department of Health and Human Services are busy at work revising the Bush, "Just Say No" emphasis in sex education. They plan to add, "But if you say 'Yes' use a condom." The Federal Government has already spent over two billion dollars for sex education programs that caused more problems than they solved, and amazingly, they are planning to blow as much as seven billion more on their condom based nonsense. As parents sleep tonight the wheels in Washington are turning, pushing, a "Safe Sex Program," that rightly should be called "Dangerous Sex," or even "Deadly Sex," down our throats.

The picture is indeed grim; but there is hope. We cannot wait for our government to figure out why their plan isn't working. If they still don't get it, they might never. We have to move ourselves, and move decisively and do it today.

The Answer

I first learned of this exciting solution to America's sexual dilemma, as I learn of so many things, from Dr. James Dobson's

Focus On The Family Ministry. Without broadcast and written ministries like those led by James Dobson, Pat Robertson, and Beverly LaHaye our government could operate like a thief in the night, and destroy our rights to express our beliefs or practice our faith.

The Southern Baptist Sunday School Board has initiated a program called *True Love Waits.* The program urges teens to sign a 3" x 5" pledge card, promising to "remain sexually pure from this moment on." The goal of the program is to collect 500,000 cards. What a message! In Dr. Dobson's October 1993 Newsletter he reported these organizations as having shown interest in this program:

Fellowship Of Christian Athletes
National Institute of Youth Ministries
Church of God (Cleveland)
Pentecostal Church Of God
National Conference Of Chatholic Bishops
Josh McDowell Ministries
The American Family Association
Youth For Christ
Assemblies Of God
Reach Out Ministries
Student Discipleship
Youth With A Mission
The 700 Club

When I first read about this program it gave me the kind of adrenaline rush I used to get before I ran out on a football field, or jumped out of an airplane. This time the rush came from an absolute understanding that:

- The condom-based nonsense is too stupid a plan to survive any longer than 1996 (when we Americans will fire its Authors).
- We have, thanks to the innovative Baptists, something that can and will work.

I predict that the *True Love Waits* program is only the beginning of a nationwide movement of parents to rescue their children from the safe sex mythology.

A Battleplan for Parents

A man, for whom I have tremendous respect, and hope that he will be a key player in bringing our nation back to sanity is William Bennett. In 1987, then Secretary of Education, Bennett wrote a twenty-eight page booklet titled *AIDS And The Education Of Our Children: A Guide For Parents And Teachers*. The booklet should still be available from the Consumer Information Center, Department Ed., Pueblo, Colorado 81009. Mr. Bennett suggests four ways that schools and parents can be taught restraint in sexual activity. The following is an outline of those four points, and I believe, a great starting place for parents and teachers who want to become responsible leaders of our children.

1. **Help children develop clear standards of right and wrong**. Teach restraint as a virtue. Present sex education within a moral context. Speak up for the institution of the family. Set clear and specific rules regarding behavior.

2. **Set good examples.**Demonstrate moral standards through personal behavior. Demonstrate responsibility for others in personal relationships.

3. **Help children resist social pressures to engage in dangerous activities**. Encourage students to set a good example for their peers.

4. **Instruct children about AIDS**. Teach about sex in a way that emphasizes the reasons for abstinence, restraint and responsibility. (Sexual intimacy should be presented as more than merely a physical or mechanical act.)

Special Note: An extremely helpful resource in compiling the information in this Chapter, and a comprehensive and compelling argument to support the ideas in this Chapter are contained in the October 1990 edition of the *Journal of the American Family Association*, at P.O. Drawer 2440, Tupelo, Mississippi 38803.

Chapter 8

Abortion, a Matter of Convenience

The Infamous Slippery, Downhill Slide

Want to irritate a Liberal? Talk about the "slippery, downhill slide." They can't stand to hear about it, probably because they are annoyed by the truth. The slippery, downhill slide law (Law, not theory!) is that once society allows a major slippage in its collective morality, then the inevitable slide downhill has begun, and is, short of Divine intervention, almost unstoppable.

An examination of the erosion of the American perception of abortion during the past thirty years provides an excellent example of this phenomena.

From Guttmacher's Observations to High School Cheerleading

In 1961, Dr. Alan F. Guttmacher, M.D., President of Planned Parenthood Federation of America, along with Winfield Best and Frederick S. Jaffe, had a book published titled *Planning Your Family: The Complete Guide To Birth Control, Overcoming Infertility, Sterilization, With A Special Section On Abortion.* The tone of the text is set with the warning printed in the opening pages:

"This book has been prepared for persons twenty-one years of age or older, or married, who are seeking birth control information on the advice of a physician or to meet a specific health need . . . ."

Dr. Guttmacher didn't say it, but the implication is very strong that if you are under twenty-one and or unmarried, you should talk to your . . . Who? . . . parents perhaps? Keep in mind that this is the same Planned Parenthood that today uses public service announcements on the radio, presented in a conspiratorial tone, that assure kids that if they don't want to talk to their parents about "sex problems," they can always talk to those wonderful folks down at your local Planned Parenthood office.

In his chapter on Abortion, Dr. Guttmacher described the procedure for obtaining what he called a "therapeutic" abortion (therapeutic, according to Dr. Guttmacher means preformed in a hospital by a physician). The Doctor wrote:

"Hospitals have created various mechanisms to screen applicants for therapeutic abortions . . . . In many hospitals a formal board is established to evaluate these cases. The board is often composed of the head of obstetrics and gynecology, and several other heads of departments, such as psychiatry, surgery, medicine and pediatrics. The facts in each case are presented in writing to the board, and . . . the operation is permitted only when all members agree unanimously that it should be done. . . . "

Dr. Guttmacher advised his readers to avoid states with strict laws, and if they couldn't arrange for a "therapeutic abortion," to establish a medical relationship with a physician in Israel or Switzerland.

Consider the limitations that we, as a people, imposed on women attempting to destroy their children before birth. That was 1961. The final sentence of Dr. Guttmacher's chapter on abortion reveals a longing for relaxed restrictions on abortions. He wrote:

"I am afraid, however, that the advice medicine can offer such women will remain pitiful until all of us demand abortion laws adequate to meet modern family needs and to permit physicians to practice modern medicine."

I can't help but wonder if Dr. Guttmacher had any idea of the magnitude of the downhill slide into national disgrace that he and his buddies at the Planned Parenthood Federation of America were launching. Do you truly believe that the following is an example of a physician "practicing modern medicine?"

Dr. Nareshkumar Patel failed in his attempt to burn a garbage bag containing 173 babies (Of course, the newspaper article used the word "Fetuses.") Two fisherman found the bag, on a farm thirty-five miles east of Oklahoma City.

District Attorney Miles Zimmerman said, "Our research at this point indicates at the most a misdemeanor and even then it may be marginal." The law in Oklahoma justifies Dr. Patel's actions as long as none of the victims are older than twenty-four weeks.

In another case in Houston one high school girl was not allowed to participate on the high school cheerleading team because she was pregnant. Another girl was suspended from cheerleading because she had had an abortion. Predictably, the ACLU defended the girl who had had an abortion, stating that having an abortion was included in the child's First Amendment, Freedom of Speech Rights.

Witness the Downhill Slippery Slide

1961–Abortions allowed in hospitals only after submission of a written request, and the unanimous approval of a hospital board. New York had a typical U.S. law allowing abortion only if the life of the mother was endangered.

1993–Abortion defended on the right to lead cheers.

Is the End in Sight?

How far downhill have we come? You decide.

- Christians Masquerading as Abortionists. The Reverend Jessie Jackson appeared at a National Organization Of Woman Rally and spoke on behalf of The Christian Coalition For Abortion. (A Christian-Abortionist is an oxymoron. There is no such thing as a Christian-Abortionist.)

- 171 babies are killed in America every hour by so-called abortions.
- 4,400 babies are killed each day in America by so-called abortions.
- 1,600,000 babies are killed in America each year by so-called abortions.
- 30,000,000 babies have been killed in America by so called abortions since abortion on demand was legalized by Roe vs. Wade in 1973.
- 30 percent of all babies conceived in America are killed by so-called abortion.
- Abortion is *Politically Correct* in America. Consider its cheerleaders. In April, 1989, Pro Abortion Forces conducted a "Death March" (At least they named their rally appropriately) in Washington. You will recognize some of these names on the honor roll of marchers for death: Jane Fonda. Glenn Close. Ellen Burstyn. Veronica Hameel. Cybill Shepherd. Susan Sarandon. Morgan Fairchild. Donna Mills. Mary Crosby. Leonard Nimoy. Meryl Streep. Peter, Paul and Mary, and of course, that Perenial Poster Boy of Political Correctness, Phil Donahue.

Mental Gymnastics and the Abortion Mentality

Major rethinking, or mental gymnastics, are required to accept the killing of 1.6 million babies in America each year. To support abortion one must go against scientific fact, and accept the totally false supposition that a fetus is not human. The baby in the womb is never, ever called that, but always referred to as tissue mass or a fetus. It makes it much easier to justify the destruction of that "tissue mass," than it does to justify the killing of a baby.

How in the world can millions of American run roughshod over the fact that Abortion means killing babies? They cannot. They can, however, manage to support the myth of what an abortion actually is, if they can master the mental manipulations required to perceive unborn babies as "tissue masses."

True crusaders for the lives of the unborn are Dr. and Mrs. J.C. Willke. In his book *Abortion and Slavery: History Repeats,* Dr. Willke compares the Dread Scott decision, justifying slavery, to the Roe vs. Wade decision, justifying Abortion. These are the similarities he presented:

- In both cases the decision of the Court was based on a 7–2 vote.
- In each case the slave and the baby were assigned the status of non-persons.
- In each case the slave and the baby were assigned the status of property of the slaveholder and the mother respectively.
- In each case the slaveholder could buy or sell his slave, and the mother could keep or kill her baby.
- In each case the abolitionists and the pro-lifers were advised not to impose their will on the "owners."
- In each case an immoral act was assigned all of the privileges of a Legal act in America.

An Expansion of the Abortion Mentality

Coercive Abortion is a reality in Communist China. The State determines how many children a family may have, and all other pregnancies are ended in abortion. Remember the Downhill Slide law? How great a leap is it from deciding to kill your own baby to deciding to kill someone else's? The underlying belief, that life is trivial compared to the convenience of whoever holds the most power, is identical in all abortions.

Infanticide accounts for the deaths of millions of babies in India and the Orient each year. This is just a notch or two downhill from abortion. In infanticide the parents wait until after birth to decide whether to destroy or to keep their child. Often the decision is made on something as trivial as the sex of the child (Girls are most often victims, since boys are perceived to be more productive providers for the family.) The babies are often simply placed on a high shelf in the home, and allowed to starve to death. After human beings have made the jump from abortion to infanticide, where must they stop? Could we perhaps some day see parents decide to **"abort"** their children based on poor grades in school, or misbehavior?

Euthanasia is yet another direction we can choose to go once we accept human life as a disposable commodity. I believe Dr. Jack Kevorkian, also known as Dr. Death, kills his patients. Of course, he sugar coats the killing, calling it Medicide.

(Dr. Kevorkian has lost the right to prescribe medicine, and no longer uses his infamous "suicide machine" which administers a lethal drip solution to his victims.) Once I heard him criticize those involved with medicine from Hippocrates to the AMA. Hippocrates was the author of the oath Kevorkian took to become a Doctor of Medicine. In the oath he promised to "do no harm." I can't imagine doing more harm to a victim, . . . patient, than killing him.

Consider the death of one of Dr. Kevorkian's patients, Hugh Gale. Hugh was 70 years old, (Other victims of the doctor have been 43, 44, 46, and 47 years old) had emphysema and heart disease, and was killed on February 15, 1993. The doctor left some incriminating evidence behind at the scene of this crime. He filled out what he called a Final Action Form, and left it in the garbage at Mr. Gale's home. According to Kevorkian's own account this is what happened. Gale asked that the mask used to deliver carbon monoxide be removed. Gale made that request about 45 seconds after it had first been applied. The mask was removed, and then put back on the patient's face. The doctor recorded:

"In about 30–35 seconds he again flushed, became agitated . . . and immediately after saying, 'Take it off' once again, he fell into unconsciousness. . . .The mask was then left in place. . . ."

Prosecutor Carl J. Marlinga said that the evidence, "suggests that the death was involuntary and that at the last minute the patient changed his mind."

Kevorkian suggested once that he will debate critics "if they will allow themselves to be strapped to a wheelchair for 72 hours so they can't move, be catheterized and placed on the toilet, then fed and bathed." Ben Mattlin of Los Angeles wrote a letter to the editor of Time magazine, responding to Kevorkian's challenge, "Well that just about describes my life for every one of my thirty years because of a neuromuscular disease from birth." Being quadriplegic is most certainly not a fate worse than death. Mr. Mattlin wants to live.

Kevorkian's attorney, Jeoffrey Fieger compared Kevorkian to Martin Luther King and India's Mahatma Gandhi. All I want to say about that display of liberal non-thought is "Thank God, that Kevorkian wasn't the physician for Dr. King or Gandhi."

Doing Voices

My radio program was not a low budget affair. It was a no-budget deal from day one. Not being able to afford prestigious guests, or even long distance phone calls, I improvised. I did voices of people approximating the views I wanted to debunk.

One of my most frequent voices was that of Eldon C. Kicklighter, an imaginary ultra-Liberal who thought that Bill Clinton was a moderate (and still does). To get into the mood for "interviewing" Eldon, I just scratched my stomach while chewing on a long blade of grass. The following is a conversation I had with Eldon after I had been talking for half the program about Dr. Kevorkian:

Eldon: Yo! Marvin! You have just given me a great idea.

Me: I'm afraid to ask. Really, I am.

Eldon: Well, we can really cash in on this Dr. Death idea.

Me.   Cash in?

Eldon: Sure. Now think about it. Every good idea in this
          country during the past forty years became better
          idea when one thing was added to it. Know what
          that one thing is, Marvin?

Me: I haven't got a clue.

Eldon: Well, Mr. Smarty, it's drive-thru windows, that's
          what.

Me.   What has this to do with Dr. Kevorkian?

Eldon: Marvin, wake up and smell the dairy farm, son.
          We can get us a chain of drive-thru Euthanasia
          joints. Think about it!

Me: I'm afraid to.

Eldon: Marvin, we can take a deserted Dairy Queen and
          turn that baby into a Dr. Jack's Drive-Thru Pain
          Relief Clinic.

Me: You have a problem, Eldon. The customers won't
          be able to actually drive "Thru." What will you do
          with their cars if they drive up to the window,
          and are killed on the spot?

Eldon: I've thought of that too. We'll have a used car lot
          adjacent to the Clinic.

Eldon always takes things to ridiculous extremes, but he
also makes people think. If we start killing people because we
think it's a great idea, will we reach a point of Euthanasia for
people having bad-hair days? Before you dismiss this idea of
more downhill sliding, consider what happened in Holland.

Land of Wooden Shoes and Lethal Medicine

Dr. D. Alan Shewmon, M.D., wrote in the January 1988 edition of the California Physician, about euthanasia in Holland.

"The Netherlands' experience has already demonstrated the rapidity with which euthanasia for terminal illness evolves into euthanasia-on-demand, and the courts' impotence in preventing multiple flagrant abuses in a climate of legalized euthanasia."

"Euthanasia-on-Demand!" Does that sound like something we've heard before in America? It gets worse, but then with downhill sliding, it always does.

Dr. Ivan de Sluis, M.D. wrote in the 1989 Spring edition of Issues In Law And Medicine

"Indeed, it is not only more or less voluntary euthanasia that is practiced in Holland. Involuntary euthanasia is quite common, and is discussed and defended in medical journal . . . .

"In the Spring of 1985 in a nursing home at the Hague, a suspicion arose that twenty-one men and women had been killed. The Doctor admitted that he had ended the lives of six of them. He had not asked for their consent. He thought he had a right to act as he did, because they each had made a remark a year, or in some instances, four years before their death. "I do not want to become a vegetable," one of them had said. All of a sudden, the Doctor would send a patient who had made such a remark to the sickbay. There he would give the patient, whether he was ill or not, a huge amount of sedatives, so that he lost consciousness. He would then kill the now comatose patient with a generous dose of insulin . . . ."

What I have described here are not the abuses of euthanasia in Holland, but its uses. In other words, use and abuse have gradually and imperceptibly merged into one another.

Former U.S. Surgeon General C. Everett Koop observed, " . . . the practice of euthanasia in Holland has overstepped the guidelines and the standards originally agreed upon by the

Netherlands Medical Society. In a few short years, second opinions about the need for euthanasia have been abandoned . . . . All evidence in these matters is under the control of the physician, and patients have been killed without having requested death."

Involuntary euthanasia? Think about what that really means! Its just a slick way of saying "murder."

Final Exit

Derek Humphry is a former member of the Hemlock Society, a group of people who believe that suicide is a great method of problem-solving. In view of the bad news we all hear each day, I would not recommend that anyone plan on any long term relationships with any of the Hemlock Society Members.

In Mr. Humphries best selling book *Final Exit*, (Can you believe that a how-to book on suicide was a best-seller?) a list of ways to kill oneself was given. Within weeks of the book's release several people had bought the book, and demonstrated that some of the author's techniques worked. Unfortunately, no one who successfully used any of Mr. Humphries techniques is available for comment.

New York City's Cornell Medical Center published a study in a November, 1993 issue of The New England Journal of Medicine, that examined the influence of the book *Final Exit*. They reviewed the deaths of 144 New York City suicides by techniques that were suggested in the book. At least fifteen of the victims had consulted the book.

The Common Thread

Abortion has become a common means of contraception. Planned Parenthood consistently boasts of decreasing birth rate among teenagers, while downplaying the pregnancy rates. The reason is obviously a greater reliance on abortion to contribute to the:

- Convenience of pregnant teenagers.
- Money generated by Planned Parenthood.

Euthanasia is becoming a cause for many, and we have a how-to book on suicide that made the best-seller list.

The common thread is that killing all demands a trivilization of the sanctity of human life. If human life is something to destroy at the first indication of inconvenience in our society, then who will survive?

Counter-Indications

You rarely hear about the emotional trauma associated with an abortion. With an alarming percentage of teenage girls receiving two, three and even four abortions, you have to wonder what those events will mean once that person matures, and realizes the significance of their complacency. The emotional effects on a mother are only the tip of the proverbial iceberg. I wonder how many girls are led to receive abortions as easily as having a cavity filled in a tooth. (Actually abortion is a lot easier to obtain than a dental procedure. A dental procedure requires parental permission.)

Here are some of the risks in choosing abortion as a form of contraception. The statistics are taken from *Challenge To Be Pro-Life* by John Lippis.

- Laceration of the cervix . . . 4.5%
- Perforation of the uterus (causes peritonitis) . . . usually 1/2–1%, ranging up to 2.7%
- Infection, from mild to fatal . . . 2–28%
- Sterility, usually 2.5%
- First Trimester miscarriages are double to triple the normal incidence for women who have had an abortion.
- Second Trimester miscarriages are two-to-six times more likely.
- Prematurity increases forty percent after one abortion and seventy percent after two.

- Ectopci (Tubal) pregnancies increase 400–800%.
- Neonatal Deaths increase 200-400% after an abortion.

In the Fall of 1993, the link between abortion and breast cancer received national notice in our country. Some of the documentation for that connection had been available for decades. In the rush to "market" abortions the victims (mothers) are not being told the facts.

Astonishing

I believe it is truly astonishing what the people who are marketing abortions will not tell you. Anything that paints the picture of their action, for what it really is, is censored.

Much of the truth about abortions concerns the violence of the acts. The babies can feel the immense pain of these barbaric procedures. Here are descriptions taken from the booklet, *Live And Let Live*, the program for the 1991 State Educational Conference of the New Mexico Right to Life Committee.

Suction Abortion:

Used in most abortions during the first three weeks of pregnancy, the mouth of the womb (cervix) must be dilated. Next a suction curette (hollow tube with a knife-like edged tip) is inserted into the womb. A strong suction then tears the baby to pieces, drawing them into a container.

Dilation and Curettage (D&C):

This method is often used in the first thirteen weeks of pregnancy. A sharp knife-like instrument, a curette, is inserted into the womb through the dilated cervix. The abortionist then scrapes the wall of the uterus, cutting the baby's body into pieces.

Dilation and Evacuation (D&E):

This method is usually used between three to four months, requiring that the abortionist dismember the baby before grasping forceps. The developing baby is removed from the womb piece by piece. In some cases, the head is too large and must be crushed in order to remove it. Bleeding is often profuse.

Because it involves the physician and staff manually destroying and handling the fetal head, arms and legs, the D&E method is particularly traumatic to those who preform them; many nurses refuse to assist in the D&E abortions because of their gruesome nature.

Abortion advocates are promoting the D&E procedure because it ensures the baby's death, unlike the second trimester abortion methods (i.e. saline or prostaglandin) where the child may be born alive.

Saline Injection (Salt Poisoning):

The procedure used for second trimester and sometimes third trimester abortions is accomplished by injecting a salt solution into the amniotic sac. The baby breathes and swallows the solution and usually dies one to two hours later from salt poisoning, dehydration, hemorrhages of the brain and other organs, and convulsions. The baby's skin is often burned off by the salt solution. Then, about 24 to 48 hours later, the mother goes into labor and delivers a dead or dying baby.

Prostaglandin Abortion:

During the second half of pregnancy, a hormone like compound is often injected into the muscle of the uterus, causing it to contract intensely, thereby pushing out the developing baby. Many babies have been born alive during this procedure.

Hysterotomy or Cesarian Section Abortion:

Used during the sixth to ninth month of pregnancy, the abdomen and the womb are opened surgically, the baby is lifted out and allowed to die by neglect or sometimes killed by direct action.

Don't You Just Wish

As I typed those last paragraphs, I needed to get up and walk around, to take some deep breaths, and to work on myself, just to keep from getting sick. Now if I had been writing about an ugly tumor being "cut to pieces," "crushed" or etc, typing those words would have had little effect on me. The point is that those words describe in vivid detail what is being done to 1.6 million American babies each year.

Don't you just wish that we could wire up some of those fervent abortionists to some lie detection apparatus, and have them read about the real truth of what abortion actually is. Then, in between each description, we could ask them to say, while the lie detector monitored their bodily functions, "We are only talking about the removal of a fetus, and not the taking of a human life." Don't you just wish?

Origins in Hatred

It should be no surprise that the founding sister of Planned Parenthood, Margaret Sanger had taken notes from that master of hatred Karl Marx. Margaret wrote for the Socialist newspaper *The Call* for a while, and, as most devotees of Marx, she spent a great deal more energy in bashing those objects of her hatred than she did championing anyone. Ms. Sanger was especially passionate in her hatred of racial minorities. It is consistent with her ideology that the organization she founded is probably doing more today to destroy racial minorities in America than the Klu Klux Klan will ever approach. Sanger called for "Social regeneration," and the "elimination of human weeds."

In Linda Gordon's book *Woman's Body, Woman's Right: A Social History of Birth Control In the United States,* (1974), Ms. Sanger is quoted as having spoken about the "Negro Project" she launched in 1939.

"The mass of Negroes, particularly in the South, still breed carelessly and disastrously, with the result that the increase among Negroes, even more than among whites, is from that portion of the population least intelligent and fit."

Temporarily, Planned Parenthood has stopped the public bashing of blacks. (Now they're truned to the support of Abortion.) Today, Planned Parenthood has new groups to hate, groups like parents and Christians.

Don't Get Caught

You can easily get caught in a trap speaking out against abortion, especially when you consider the eligibility of pro-choice political candidates. You might even be called one of the dreaded "one issue voters." Liberals usually enunciate "one issue voters" while pointing an extended index finger toward the base of their throat. If you stop thinking while watching network news, even you could begin to think that there was something inherently wrong with being a "one issue voter."

Remember that the issue is the mass taking of human life. Undoubtedly many people supported Adolph Hitler because he ended inflation, the depression, unemployment and really got the German people pulling together. As for that annoying thing he had about sending trainloads of Jewish men, women and children to gas chambers, well, you wouldn't want to be a one issue voter, would you? If the issue is important enough to you, to determine who you will or will not vote for, nobody has the right to minimize your interest in that issue. While you're thinking about this one, think about all of the Americans who vote solely on the basis of the fact that their candidate endorses something that brings them money.

If you can get hold of a history book that hasn't been revised by some liberal historians, you can prove that this country was colonized because of a single issue, freedom of religion. You will also find that our greatest war was fought over one single issue, and coincidentally, that issue concerned whether or not a group of people qualified as human beings.

One issue! So what? Its your vote. Its your right to cast it anyway you choose. Besides, there are candidates who think a lot like you think. I recall a real president by the name of Reagan who said on July 3, 1988, "If America is to remain what God, in His wisdom, intended for it to be—a refuge, a safe haven for those seeking basic human rights—then we must once again extend the most basic human right to the most vulnerable members of the human family. We must commit ourselves to a future in which the right to life of every human being—no matter how weak, no matter how small, no matter how defenseless—is protected by our laws and public policy."

By the way, I am a one-issue voter, and I'm proud of it. I am certain that I, as a citizen of this great nation, deserve to be led by a man or woman who at least has the human decency to defend the most defenseless among us. I'll have a candidate who defends the right to life. I'll demand it. That is the way a democracy works. God bless America, and protect our unborn.

Chapter 9

America, a Multi-Cultural Mess?

Today I watched Good Morning America. The program was being broadcast from Puerto Rico. One young woman, who looked and talked like a college student was asked what she thought of the national celebrations taking place in her country. She said "Puerto Rico has a five hundred year history of oppression and sadness." Then she added, "That is what we are."

People who buy that overworked "I am a victim, woe is me!" malarkey should be required to put it on their resumés. Could you imagine?

Experience: 500 years of oppression and sadness.

Professional Objective: To continue to contribute to my people's five hundred years of oppression and sadness.

Job Title: Oppressed sad person.

As I listened to that young woman I felt a slow, bubbling rage for the teachers who put their 500 year burden of imaginary angst on her shoulders. I couldn't help but wish that every college student in America who has been infected with that kind of philosophy would be required to spend an equal amount of time in a classroom with someone like motivational speaker Les Brown. Les is one of millions of Americans who happened to have been born into a minority race, and happened to be raised in poverty, and had multitudinous reasons for rage, but, he made a momentous decision to make something spectacular out of himself.

The difference between a dynamic, happy, well adjusted, and incredibly productive and successful human being like Les Brown, and that beautiful young Puerto Rican girl, is nothing more than a tiny shift in focus. There probably was a time when Les, an abandoned child growing up in inner city Miami's infamous Liberty City, a time when he took a deep breath, and said to himself "I want to do something special with my life." The most magnificent thing about Les Brown is that he takes his learnings, and helps other human beings.

Baseball, Apple Pie and Victimhood

The new great American past time is finding someone, or some group, to blame for all of your problems. The pastime extends from the couches of our therapists to our foreign policy.

A couple of years ago I heard a psychologist make an incredible statement. He said that all of the people he had ever encountered who were overweight, had been sexually abused.

Sex abuse and obesity are often related but for someone to make a statement like that is preposterous. Two years later I first heard of a growing group in America called, the False Memory Support Group. Most of these people are parents of children who have falsely accused them of sexual abuse. The accusers probably aren't telling out-and-out-lies, but after what amounts to coercion from therapists who suspect (or intend to discover) sexual abuse, the accusers "remember" the sexual abuse they had "blocked out." The confusion comes from the real fact that sexual abuse is often blocked out of the conscious memory, but the therapist-led witch hunts are bound to uncover phantom memories that do nothing but cause great and unnecessary pain to the accused. The search through the memory banks for these "abusers" is typical of a society that is ever vigilant for a new place to dump massive doses of blame.

While finding the abuser(s) helps the patient to make sense of "dysfunctional" behavior, they continue the avoidance dance and maneuver away from responsibility.

Marxism: The Edsel of Political Systems

Listen to what the people leading the left wing organizations such as the National Organization of Women (NOW) or the National Education Association(NEA) or the American Civil Liberties Union (ACLU) or Planned Parenthood have to say. After a while it all sounds the same. That's because much of it originated from the very same man. His name was Karl Marx.

Socialism is based on some of the nastiest appraisals of humankind ever written. Marx, Engels and Lenin were hate filled men. The founders of nearly all of the major liberal anti-God, anti-family, anti-people movements were disciples of Marx, et. al.

Liberation is a word common to socialist writings. Its no coincidence that the early feminist movement was called the Woman's Liberation Movement. Pathfinder Books published a series of books and booklets on the Woman's Liberation Movement from a Marxist Perception—Two of those books are *Feminism And The Marxist Movement,* by Mary Alice Waters in 1972 and *Sexual Politics: A Marxist Appreciation* by Kate Millett in 1971.

The NEA has held a One World Order agenda for decades. In the January 1946 edition of the NEA Journal, Joy Elmer Morgan wrote in an editorial titled *The Teacher and World Government.*

"In the struggle to establish an adequate world government, the teacher has many parts to play. . . . He can do much to prepare the hearts and minds of children for Global understanding and cooperation. . . . At the very top of all the agencies which will assure the coming of world government must stand the school, the teacher, and the organized profession." (Perhaps you have been wondering why so many American children are functionally illiterate. The "teachers" are too busy getting them ready for world government to teach them how to read.)

U.S. News and World Report estimates that there are 10,000 Marxist professors teaching Socialism in American Colleges and Universities. What is Socialism? Ask a Russian who lost all of his land because the State suddenly outlawed ownership of private property. Better still, ask a Hungarian why his parents and grandparents gave their lives so that their children wouldn't have to live under this system.

To appreciate the "rules of the game" for Socialists, consider this quotation from Lenin:

"One must be prepared to make all kinds of sacrifices and overcome the greatest obstacles in order to propagandize and agitate systematically, stubbornly, persistently, and patiently, precisely in those institutions, associations, and unions, even the most reactionary, where there is a proletarian or semi-prolatarian mass. . . one must be prepared . . . in case of necessity, even to resort to all kinds of tricks and ruses, to employ illegal measures, secretiveness, and concealment of truth in order to penetrate into trade unions, to remain in them, and to conduct Communist work in them at any cost."

The preceding quotation was excerpted from the book, *The Country of the Blind: The Soviet System of Mind Control* by George S. Count and Nucia Lodge, (1949).

The primary target of liberal groups is that all-time, worst enemy of mankind, that scourge of the planet, that one and only one world class villain *the white male*. The second worst people in the world, according to Liberals, are family members of white male-led families, especially if they are Christians.

Diversity Consultants

Diversity, as espoused by many Liberals today, is not diversity, but, divisiveness. The idea behind the Diversity Movement or multi-culturalism is to celebrate differences in people, differences in race, creed, religion and sexual orientation. The actual effect is that white males are bashed by all sub cultures, blamed for all existing problems, and, in some cases, demanded to make up for the real or imagined abuses of their ancestors. Diversity is the word used by Liberals, but divisiveness is what they achieve.

Similarities in their philosophies are:

- Universal blame placing for all problems.
- Tremendous energy expanded identifying selves as victims.
- Having chosen the role of victims, denial or condemnation of individual achievement by group members.
- Action plans are based on hatred, devoting a preponderance of efforts to bashing others, as opposed to elevation of esteem through increased accomplishments of the group and its members.
- A lot of "getting even" behavior, punishing others (usually white males) as if the pain of others elevated members of any other group(s).
- Refusal of the group to take responsibility for anything. If large numbers of group members riot, the leadership will predictably contend that it was justified because of "oppression."
- Refusal to censor any behavior of one's own group, no matter how inappropriate.

Race Relations or Racism

In 1972 I managed, after a considerable effort, to persuade my Commanding Officer to send me to the eleven week training program known as the Defense Race Relations Institute, or DRRI, at Patrick Air Force Base in Florida. That school represented the most extensive effort in the world to actually teach people how to make positive changes in the field of race relations.

I was a motivated Race-Relations Officer. I grew up in Birmingham, Alabama, a city some people believe synonymous with racial hatred. In my segregated childhood I had my parents and teachers give me some pretty flaky answers to questions, questions like, "Why do they have 'White' and 'Colored' signs over water fountains in stores?" The answer I received then was, "They are dirty." Later, in places like Vietnam, I learned that there were good men, really fine and sterling individuals in all races. I attacked the Race-Relations Assignment with a missionary zeal.

In the '70s we enforced quotas, and at the time quotas made sense to me. I still do believe that, for that time, with a system that had been administered so unfairly, that quotas were a way to bring about equity in an expedient and fair manner. It took a black Sergeant Major to teach me something I never heard mentioned at DRRI. The Sergeant Major stopped me inside his Battalion area, and invited me to his office. He then told me that he didn't appreciate what I was doing. He detested the idea of black soldiers being promoted to fill quotas. I asked him why, and he wasn't a bit bashful in telling me. He said, "I worked hard for my stripes. It took me twenty-six years to get that star," pointing to the star in the middle of six stripes on his fatigue jacket.

"The quota system makes my star look cheap," continued the Sergeant Major. "These soldiers should have to earn their rank, just like I earned mine."

Then the Sergeant Major said something that makes as much good sense today as it did twenty years ago. He said, "quotas are racist." I had no idea what he meant by that remark. He explained, "A quota says to the world, 'Hey, look at these black soldiers. The only way to promote them is to force them into jobs they aren't qualified to do. Enforcing quotas is like saying we are going to promote these men the only way we can, "by faking it."

I then tried to argue with him saying, "Their rank is real. What do you mean calling it 'fake.'"

"Real?" he bellowed. "You go get yourself a truckload of those quota Sergeant Majors and bring them here to see me. I am a *real* Sergeant Major. I'll go up against any of those guys on knowledge, experience or the ability to get things done. My rank was wasn't a *gift*. I earned it. I earned it because I was the best soldier for the job."

The Sergeant Major then said something else about quotas that made a lot of sense. He said, "If you have to have quotas anywhere in the Army, put them in schools. Send the younger soldiers to schools so that when they get the rank they'll know what to do with it."

The Sergeant Major's Rules for Racism

Any time I hear of a new program for racial equality I apply what I think of as the Sergeant Major's Rules for Racism to the project. These are the kinds of questions he would demand to have answered before he would approve of a "program."

1. Will the program draw attention to a minority, and presuppose that they could not achieve on their own what they are being given?
2. Will members of the minority who have already achieved whatever is being given away experience a diminished status?
3. Will the people being promoted or favored be ready to accept the new responsibilities of the promotion or favor?

Nuainces of Racism

While I served as the race Relations Officer for the 2nd Armored Division at Fort Hood, Texas, I was often supervised by my Reviewing Officer, Brigader General Willard O. Dillard. General Dillard was, in 1974, one of a growing group of black General Officers in the Army. General Dillard and I both came from

Birmingham, but because of segregation we had both been raised in half a city. Neither of us knew anything about the side of town where the other had been raised.

General Dillard once told me that detecting real die-hard racists was relatively simple. The whites, a step or two removed from the clan, did little to disguise their behavior. The more militant blacks were as obvious in their behavior. The General then said that what he wanted me to deal with more energetically was what he called the "subtle nuances" of racism. It was several years later that an incident reminded me of how damaging the subtle nuances of racism could be.

Bobby's Raw Deal

I first met Bobby (not his real name) while I was serving as the Director of Housing in a community college in the Southwest. Bobby was a black student from inner city Detroit. He was a kid with the world on a string. Bobby was President of the student body, and Captain of the basketball team. Bobby was a handsome young man, who made friends about every time he shook hands.

One night Bobby stopped by my room, and asked a favor. He said that he had heard that I was a writer, and wanted to know if I would help him out with his English Composition. I said, "Sure, leave it with me, and I'll get back to you tomorrow."

Later that night I read Bobby's writing. It was an outrage, not on Bobby, but on the people who had conspired to trick Bobby into thinking that he had been getting an education. The kingpins of the scam had been basketball coaches. They had managed to guide Bobby for years to teachers who would pass Bobby through the system without bothering to teach him how to read and write. The tragedy was that Bobby actually thought that he was almost ready to attempt to get into law school. Bobby's writing would have been cause for alarm in a fourth grade class. Not one single person had the human decency to tell Bobby that he had a problem with writing. I attempted to tell Bobby what he needed to do (get major tutoring immediately), but he didn't believe me. Bobby probably thought that I was racist. I believe that what the educational system did collectively to Bobby was as mean and as despicable as any racist act I ever saw.

The Minority Voting Myth

Some people contend that one of President Bill Clinton's major strengths has been minority voters. There has been some truth in that belief, but thanks to Mr. Clinton's consistent anti-God, anti-family, behavior his minority strength is waning. Mr. Clinton's minority support is not based on a minority love affair with Liberalism, but with a waning loyalty to the Democratic Party.

The lead story of the October, 1993 issue of the Christian American began with the headline, *Minority Myths Exploded: Poll Shows Minorities Hold Traditional Values.* The story, written by John Wheeler and Paul English revealed such information as:

- 63 percent of Blacks and 43 percent of Hispanics, compared to 40 percent of Whites, identify themselves as "Born again Christians."
- Between 80 and 88 percent of Blacks, Hispanics and Whites favor school choice and school prayer.
- 79 percent of Whites, 62.8 percent of Hispanics and 73.4 percent of Blacks favor spending cuts in Government.
- 91.2 percent of Blacks and 85.8 percent of Hispanics believe that able-bodied welfare recipients should be required to work for their benefits.
- Only 37.6 percent of Blacks and 38.6 percent of Hispanics favored Hiring Quotas.

In spite of attempts to keep minorities illiterate by lowering educational standards to a point of near non existence, more and more minorities are reading. They are reading and learning. They are learning about the source of the real threat to the things they hold most dear, their love of God, family and, yes indeedy, Country.

Dad, Does Androgyny Have Anything to do With Haircuts?

Motivational speaker, Cavett Robert tells a story about a woman in Cavett's home town. Cavett and his grandfather were walking down a country road in a Mississippi town when they passed a woman. Cavett described the woman as the town "character." He said that his grandfather tipped his hat to the woman. Cavett asked his grandfather, "Why did you tip your hat to her? You know who she is, don't you?" Cavett's grandfather responded with "old southern wisdom." "Tipping my hat doesn't have anything to do with whether or not she is a lady. I tip my hat because I'm a gentleman."

The Femi-Nots

There are two kinds of women: feminine—also known as ladies, and those calling themselves feminists—but are not feminine at all.

One event that accentuated the differences between the ladies and the femi-nots was the First National Woman's Conference in Houston in November 1977. There were 20,000 attendees. The official report of that conference was presented to President Jimmy Carter by Bella Abzug.

One of the many speeches was made by Brenda Parker, President of Future Homemakers of America. Ms. Parker said, " . . . this conference has dealt so strongly with the roles of women and especially the homemaker."

Those words had to send shivers up the spines of the Femi-nots. The Femi-nots were not then and are not now nearly as dedicated to expanding the roles of women as they say.

At the Houston Conference there were elegant ladies like Betty Ford, Lady Bird Johnson and Rosalynn Carter. Texas delegate Anne Richards was the first to speak out for the Equal Rights Amendment.

There were also women there who hated men with far more passion than they loved women. There was Margaret Mead and Gloria Steinem who recently retracted many things she had preached during the early years of the Femi-nots.

There were twenty-five planks in the final report from the Woman's Conference. Plank number twenty-one called for "Reproductive Freedom" also known as "Abortion." Plank number twenty-three called for "Sexual Preference," also known as Lesbianism. It was over these two planks that the division between the ladies present and the Femi-nots became apparent.

There was screaming and foot stomping galore as an effort was made to stop the debate on abortion prematurely. Ann O'Donnell of Missouri spoke a few sentences against abortion that presented as sound and succinct an argument in favor of life for the unborn as you will ever hear. She said:

"It is the antithesis of the feminist movement to oppress the less-powerful. It, therefore, has to be absolutely ridiculous for people who call themselves feminists to suggest that they kill their unborn children to solve their problems."

The Reproductive Freedom Plank was passed by a standing vote that appeared to be about five to one in favor of the plank. Anti-Abortion delegates bowed their heads and prayed after the plank was passed. With the passage of that plank many pro-life women were philosophically excluded from what most Americans considered to be the mainstream Feminist Movement.

The passage of the bill on sexual preference provides a look at a pattern for the passage of Homosexual and Lesbian legislation that has been repeated often enough to be acknowledged as a definable scheme. The resolution came to the floor late at night, hours after the supper break had been skipped. The tired and hungry delegates were primed for the debate. Non-delegate Lesbians packed the bleachers. TV cameras were poised. As often occurs during debate concerning Homosexuality and Lesbianism, a "coming out" was staged. Betty Friedan said, "As someone who has grown up in Middle America and as someone who has loved men too well, I have had trouble with this issue." Two demonstrations followed passage of this plank, and those two demonstrations further identified the differences between the ladies and the Femi-nots. The Lesbians and their supporters shouted, "Thank you sisters," and released hundreds of pink and yellow balloons that said, "We are everywhere." They snake-danced across the front of the arena. At the same time Joan Gubbins gave a signal and the Mississippi Delegates opposing the plank turned their backs and bent their heads in prayer, while holding signs reading "Keep them in the closet."

Feminism has in many areas been very good for America. As a father of an athletic daughter I am pleased that my daughter received as much attention and support for her swimming achievements as did any football player at her college. That equality, that fairness, was brought about because of crusading feminists and their supporters. In 1972, I was told at the Race Relations Institute that Feminism applied to anyone who favored equality for women. Based on that definition I want to be called a Feminist.

The differences between ladies and Femi-nots was demonstrated in the Spring of 1992. C-Span covered a National Organization of Women (NOW) Rally, held on the Mall in Washington. Minutes before the rally a group of women from Beverly LaHaye's Organization, Concerned Women for America were interviewed. These women dressed as if they had just walked out of a wedding, they spoke with poise and authority on women's issues such as the right-to-life of unborn women.

They spoke for about ten minutes. They didn't need any longer than that, because they quickly got to the point. It's significant that representatives from C.W.A. were interviewed before the NOW rally because the C.W.A. membership is at least double that of the NOW. The reason many Americans believe the NOW-type women represent the woman's movement in America is because they put on a much better show by media standards, and therefore get much greater coverage than the ladies of C.W.A. Comparing NOW to the C.W.A. is, as far as the media is concerned, like comparing *Lady Chatterly's Lover* to *Alice In Wonderland.* The media will almost always choose "raunch" over style and substance.

The NOW Rally featured Lesbian Comics (Shouldn't that be an oxymoron?) telling funnies about the Pope in Drag, etc. There were women, clothed and not, "smooching" on camera, bringing crudity down to a new level. Jane Fonda and Jessie Jackson were there, and for three hours the show went on, and on, and on, until the speakers got tired and the audience was exhausted.

The Male Decision: to React or Respond

Men have the choice to react or respond to the Women's movement in America. Appreciate the difference by thinking what your doctor would mean if he said you were "reacting" to medication. If, on the other hand, he told you that you were "responding" to the medication, the meaning turns from negative to positive. Men reacting to women, are fulfilling their prophecy by participating in what could be called testosterone-driven behavior. Men who take the higher road, resist the biological drive to react, and choose a response more appropriate for all.

Reaction

Much of what has been said by the Femi-nots about and to men has been rhetorical violence. The reaction to violence is violence, and it has occurred in alarmingly increasing incidents.

As early as 1966 Patrick Moynihan, then Assistant Labor Secretary under President Johnson issued the *Moynihan Report.* In his report Mr. Moynihan pointed out that men had a drive to be the providers in their families. Fulfilling those roles gave positive channeling to male behavior. As men were systematically excluded from family life in black ghettos they were also denied a place to live out their male drives. The leadership in those ghettos shifted increasingly away from men and to mothers, and to female teachers and social workers. The male, relegated to the role as an outside observer, began to rechannel his testosterone-directed behavior in the predictable direction of violence. Also predictably, the victims of male violence have been those who are now occupying the male roles—women. Without membership and responsibility in families, males have increasingly turned to their hastily-fabricated new families, the Gangs.

What If Men Responded?

What would happen if most men in America today, responded to America's problems? What would happen if men considered all of the problems I have described in this book and said, Whoa! That's enough! What would happen?

Men are driven to *lead.* Our cavemen ancestors lead by hunting, and bringing in the food. If the hunting grounds weren't productive enough to feed the family, and the clan, men found new hunting grounds, and initiated movement.

Too many people can't praise one gender without bashing another. I'm not doing that. Not at all! Women and men simply couldn't make it without each other. They depend on each other for biological furtherance of the race, for love, for that unique teamwork that builds great families.

God always chose men to lead His peoples. He chose men like Abraham, David, Samuel, Saul, Solomon, Noah and Moses. He chose those men because they had something special, something envied by all men. They had the gift of leadership. They were appointed to lead, and they led.

America is indeed in a mess today, and the logical ones to lead us out of this mess are men. What if men were to begin to pray in great numbers? What if men were to take back the leadership roles in the family? What if men were to spiritually lock arms, and make statements through their behavior that the idiocy in this land is now stopped? What if men stood tall together, and did precisely what God intended them to do? What if men brought America back to God? What if men led the way by taking the strongest position men can assume—on their knees before God? What if men demanded sexual purity in their relationships? What if responsible "fatherhood" were to once again become one of the most noble aspirations of men? What if fathers led by doing, and disciplined themselves not to watch TV, read books or attend movies that offended their God? What if there was no need for women to fend off sexually-aggressive men, because men believed that sex was a gift reserved for married couples? What if daughters and sons looked to their fathers, knowing that unconditional love, consistent discipline, and unflinching leadership were synonymous with the word "Dad?"

America's problems appear terribly complex. The illusion of complexity exists only because men have turned their back on God, and on the very logical and always available solutions to America's problems. The solutions are not ever going to be found in condom distribution, gun-control, increased taxation, or any of the other liberal band-aids to America's enormous wounds. The solution will be found with men leading this nation back where it belongs, truly a nation *Under God*.

A Numbers Game

For decades Homosexuals touted the "statistic" that ten percent of the American population was Homosexual. Those numbers were based on Kinsey's studies of American Sexuality, and Kinsey has been exposed as a very sloppy scientist. For example, twenty-five percent of Kinsey's samples of American men were in penitentiaries. Newer, and more reliable studies indicate that the actual percentage of homosexuals in America might actually be less than one percent.

All the News That's Politically Correct

For months our nation debated the issue of whether homosexuals would have special status in the Military.

The results of a study of the issue were reported in the June 4th 1993 issue of Washington Times. The headline was *Court-Martials of Gays Usually for Sex Assaults.* The study covered the court martial proceedings of 102 military personnel between 1989 and 1992. Over eighty percent of the cases involved sexual assaults. Over half of the cases involved child molestation. More than two-thirds of the incidents occurred on bases or posts, and nearly half in a barracks setting. Sixty-two percent involved a superior using rank to facilitate crimes. Twenty-two percent involved consensual sex, but were prosecuted because of "compelling factors" such as acts occurring in public places. Five percent of the personnel involved tested positive for HIV.

The same article reported that the sex crime rate among homosexuals in the Army was 3.52 cases per thousand, while the Army wide rate was 2.45 cases per thousand.

From GRID To AIDS

The previous example of homosexual deception contributed to a negligible political advantage. This deception has and is costing many lives.

When the infamous "patient zero" was identified as a homosexual airline male steward, he was counseled by health care professionals in California. He was told that he had what was then called Gay Related Immune Deficiency, or GRID. He was told that the disease was spread through homosexual sex. The night he was told this information "patient zero" reportedly went to a San Francisco bath house and had homosexual sex with as many as twelve partners. At one time he cooperated with health officials and named over seventy men with whom he had had sex—and those were just the men whose names he could remember.

In those early days, when the disease was just beginning to spread in epidemic proportions throughout the world, the disease was called GRID because researchers knew that homosexual sex was the primary means of transmission. From the beginning there was a political effort, much of it originating in the Center for Disease Control to downplay the role of Homosexuals in the spreading of GRID. The very name of the disease was changed to throw people off the track. In those early days many homosexual activists knew what was being done, and fought to have the homosexual community better informed about their vulnerability to the disease.

These paragraphs are not about blame. With a disease as deadly as AIDS there is no time for blame. I am reporting on the vulnerability of homosexuals to the disease.

As these words are being written more information is being released about the spread of AIDS through casual contact. I interviewed Doctor Lorraine Day in 1992, regarding her book, *What The Government Isn't Telling You About AIDS*. She said then that surgical nurses had died from AIDS and their only contact had been exposure on their skin to AIDS-infected blood.

As deadly as AIDS is, information is still being altered or withheld. Dr. Day suggested that much of the responsibility for misinformation on AIDS had originated in the CDC and had been engineered by homosexuals in that organization.

A British Memorandum from the House of Commons, titled the Third Report From The Social Services Committee, Problems Associated With AIDS Volume III, Minutes Of Evidence (8 April–13 May 1987), featured on page 142 a memorandum by

Dr. John Seale of the Royal Society of Medicine. Dr. Seale wrote:

"Sexual intercourse is only one of many ways by which the virus can be transmitted, and is by no means the most efficient. . . . Male homosexual contact of the finger, penis or tongue with the rectal wall of another man transmits the virus very easily. Seventy percent of the male homosexual population of San Francisco were infected within six years of the arrival of the virus in the city. . . . The percentages are rising . . . unaffected by the highly acclaimed "safe sex" propaganda. . . . By equating sodomy with sexual intercourse the impression is given that homosexuals have just been unlucky. . . . In reality homosexual activity has spread the virus through the population at a vastly greater speed than normal sexual intercourse could achieve."

AIDS Awareness

I recently saw the Surgeon General of the United States Joycelyn Elders, on TV. Doctor Elders had a unique AIDS Awareness ribbon pinned to her blouse. It was a tiny red ribbon, about a third of the size of the ones most people wear. I think her tiny ribbon is appropriate. I don't think Doctor Elders should want to be counted among those trying to raise awareness of AIDS. Doctor Elders, and her "condom advocacy" are spreading the very disease she purports to tame. Condoms exacerbate every problem they attempt to solve. Red ribbons, to many people, are synonymous with condom distribution. These ribbons seem to say what Liz Taylor said to a crowd of 70,000 at an AIDS benefit at Wembley Stadium in London, "Protect yourselves! Every time you have sex, use a condom. Straight sex, gay sex, bisexual sex." This is the best advice the President of the American Foundation for AIDS Research could give to a crowd.

If people are really serious about stopping AIDS, it still can be done. I suggest that serious people wear white ribbons, you know, white as in purity, white as in abstinence. If we promoted abstinence we would all be much closer to the solution to the AIDS problem.

Chapter 10

One Nation Under God?

In 1962, God was officially removed from our Nation's public schools. For over two hundred years our nation had buzzed along with virtually no problems concerning the interpetation of the first amendment. Then the silliness began. If it weren't that the silliness offended God almighty, and has very obviously affected the welfare of the Nation in a most negative way, this would all be chalked up to political absurdity. Observe the court cases since 1962, and witness the march of silliness.

- Prayer, recited aloud, even if it is voluntary and denominationally neutral, is unconstitutional.
  Engel vs. Vitale 1962.
- Freedom of speech doesn't count if the subject is religious.
  Stein vs. Oshinsky, 1965.
- A student can't pray aloud before a meal.
  Beed vs. van Hoven, 1965.
- Kindergarten students can't recite, "We thank you for the flowers so sweet; We thank you for the food we eat; We thank you for the birds that sing; We thank you for everything;" even though "God" isn't mentioned, those words might be considered prayer.
  DeSpain vs. DeKalb County Community School District, 1967.
- A war memorial can't be designed in the shape of a cross.
  Lowe vs. City of Eugene, 1969.
- A board of Education can't refer to "God" in any of its writings.
  State of Ohio vs. Whisner, 1976.

- Kindergarten children are forbidden to ask whose birthday is celebrated on Christmas.
  Florey vs. Sioux Falls School Dist.1979.
- The ten commandments can't be hung on the walls of a school because students might read or even obey them.
  Stone vs. Graham 1980.
- Children can't recite, "God is great. God is good.
  Let us thank Him for our food."
  Wallace vs. Jaffree 1985.
- School prayer at graduation ceremonies are unconstitutional.
  Graham vs. Central Community School District 1985.

In Las Cruces, New Mexico the American Civil Liberties Union (ACLU) threatened the school district with a law suit on behalf of one family who objected to a Christmas Play that depicted the birth of Christ. This happened in 1993, in America.

The founding Fathers had no intention of loading down our nation with this sort of silliness, and they certainly had no intention of taking God entirely out of anything remotely related to government.

If you're a parent, and you have children in public school, I strongly recommend that you read David Barton's Book *The Myth of Separation*. I also suggest that you watch Pat Robertson's 700 Club on a regular basis to keep up with the continuing attempts to exclude God and godliness from America.

The farce of defending the first amendment being led by the ACLU in America today is nothing more than a frontal assualt on Christianity. The same people who insist that Christmas be called the "Winter Holidays" will tell you they want only to keep religion out of our schools. They lie. They want to exclude the slightest mention or allusion to Jesus Christ. The same people that cry out against Religion in schools, want New Age Subjects taught. They want Greek and Roman Mythology and all the information pertaining to those ancient Gods taught. They want

Eastern religions taught. Most obviously they want the High Feast Of Satanism (Halloween) celebrated.

Here are a few of hundreds of quotes I could supply you with on how our founding fathers really felt about the role of God, and more specifically Jesus Christ, in the building and maintenance of our Government.

"Bless O Lord the whole race of mankind, and let the world be filled with the knowledge of Thee and Thy Son, Jesus Christ."—*George Washington*

"Before any man can be considered as a member of civil society, he must be considered a subject of the Governor of the Universe."—*James Madison*

"We have been assured, Sir, in the *Sacred Writings* that accept the Lord build the house, they labor in vain that build it. I firmly believe this. I also believe that, without His concurring aid, we shall succeed in this political building no better than the builders of Babel."—*Benjamin Franklin*

"God who gave us life gave us liberty. Can the liberties of a nation be secure when we have removed a conviction that these liberties are a gift of God? Indeed I tremble for my country when I reflect that God is just, and that His justice cannot sleep forever."—*Thomas Jefferson*

"It is the duty of nations, as well as of men, to own their dependence upon the overruling power of God and to recognize the sublime truth announced in the Holy Scriptures and proven by all history, that those nations only are blessed whose God is Lord."—*Abraham Lincoln*

The Action Arm of Militant Atheism in America

The ACLU sent a letter to public school officials in Tennessee, threatening them with legal action if they allowed students to pray to God during graduation ceremonies. Dewayne Oldham, principal of Westmoreland High School in Sumner County not only allowed prayer (against the threats from the ACLU and the Director of Schools) but he then sued the ACLU for sending him a misleading, intimidating and threatening letter. This kind of abuse is going on all over America. The ACLU uses intimidation, outright lies and threats to prevent anything that even hints of being a prayer or act of reverence for God.

The ACLU was founded as the Bureau for Conscientious Objectors of the American Union against Militarism in 1917. Its founder, Roger Baldwin, changed the name of the organization to the American Civil Liberties Union when he was released from prison for sedition in 1919. The original executive board was heavily peopled by leaders of the Communist Party of the USA, people like William Foster, Elizabeth Gurley Flynn and Louis Budenez. Roger Baldwin wrote papers in defense of Joseph Stalin, and said, "I am for socialism, disarmament, and ultimately for abolishing the state itself as an instrument of violence and compulsion. I seek social ownership of property. . . Communism is the goal."

The ACLU has 250,000 members, 70 staff lawyers, and 5,000 volunteer attorneys. It works on an annual budget of $14 million and handles an average of 6,000 court cases at any one time. Grace Watson Williams, the Executive Director of the ACLU in Albuquerque wrote a letter to the editor of the Las Cruces Sun News. She boasted, "This 72 year old organization has been to the U.S. Supreme Court more than any other single organization. . . ." While innocent people await trial in America our legal system is clogged with the silliness of the American Civil Liberties Union.

Here is a partial list of some of the reasons the ACLU has gone to court:
- To remove "In God We Trust" from our coins.
- To make it legal to burn the American Flag (They brag about this one in the fund raising letter they sent to me.)
- Remove Chaplains from prisons and the military.
- Legalize Child Pornography

- Tax exemption for Satanists
- Legalization of Prostitution
- Forced Busing
- Legalization of Polygamy

If you would like to meet some of these darlings of Democracy you can do so on your next trip to Washington. Just drop by the office of the former general counsel and long time member of the ACLU, Ruth Bader Ginsburg. Tell her what you think of the ACLU.

Church and State

I can shed some light on the passion that the Clinton people put on expunging God from government. I just read Texe Marrs' book *Big Sister is Watching You,* a fright-night special on Hillary Clinton. After reading the book I am certain that Hillary Clinton is running this nation, and that her beliefs are deeply rooted in New Age Fanaticism.

Author Marrs writes about how Mrs. Clinton steadfastly refused to attend the Baptist Church with Bill because it was too dogmatic. She raved over her trip to the Glide Memorial Church in San Francisco, however. The Glide Memorial Church once hosted a Hooker's Convention, is strongly pro-homosexual, and has ditched many basic Christian Doctrines. The pastor once said that he was, "tired of hearing about Jesus."

Does New Age Religion
Have Anything to do With Christianity?

The new agers occasionally mention the name of Jesus Christ. They talk of Christ as if He were God, their God. This is a deception. True new agers are not Christians.

Ten years ago I was part of the New Age Religion. I practiced hypnosis, and did past life regressions. I knew and spoke the lingo, and it all made sense to me, then. Now, I realize that the New Age Movement in America has nothing at all to do with the authentic teachings of Christ, and I also now realize the source of much of the "power" found in that religion.

Me as God?

The new agers believe that they are God. Really! They might deny it if you asked them directly, "Who do you think you are, God?" Their words, however, reveal the humongous scope of their egos.

Here are some quotes from a TV interview hosted by Mark Goodman of the Boston Men's Club in Boston, Mass. on December 28, 1988, with Michael Graham of Melbourne Australia. Mr. Graham was talking about his participation in a program called Avitar. Mr. Graham said, "Experiencing yourself as the source of your own existence is different from understanding the 'idea' that each of us is the source of our own existence. For one thing, you can make changes."

When I first heard the idea of "me as the center of my universe," it sounded good. That's it, folks. It sounds good.

The "Me as the center of my universe" stuff might sound familiar. It should. Freud described it in what he called the "King Baby Syndrome." The King Baby syndrome occurs when an infant, or infantile adult, believes the world revolves around him. The baby whose father dies, asks himself, what did I do to cause his death. The infantile nature of the New Age Belief often leads them to ask, "What did I do to bring this or that into my life." They deal with difficulty by trying to 'will' it away. Because of the serendipity happenstances of life they sometimes succeed, and proclaim their inner deity as a nifty problem solver.

Even the most generic understanding of God, as found in the twelve step programs that began with Alcoholics Anonymous, suggest that a seeker find a "Higher Power." Don't look now, new agers, but you ain't even a "Higher" power. All power in you is on loan from your Creator. Your only real control of your universe comes from a deep personal relationship with Christ, the true "Higher Power."

New Age Gimmicks

Here is a brief sampling of some of the goodies offered to the public, for a price of course, by the New Agers.

Augustin Rivas operates from a jungle clearing near the town of Tamshiyacu in northeastern Peru. Seekers travel from around the world to give Rivas about $2,000 to sit around his campfire, complain, and drink a hallucinogenic Rivas makes from vines and leaves. Rivas says, "This is not a motorcycle for the mind—it is medicine."

- For a price, the Mates Indians in Peru will blow a powder they call nu-nu through a tube and up your nostrils so that you can be treated to a "vision."

- The Mayor of Florala, Alabama, (Erh, the former mayor— he was impeached) once sprinkled a mysterious dust around City Hall, and called a midnight news conference— wearing a red turban, red bathrobe and a rubber snake around his neck to proclaim National Voodoo Week.

- Remember the NAFTA debates. I'll bet you didn't even know that Mexican Sorcerers held a debate prior to NAFTA. Jorge Jauregui, a man known as "The Goat," from Catemaco, Mexico said during a news interview, "Up there they have all kinds of inventions. . . . People could lose faith in our medicine."

- Some people attempt to contact God through the mail. Moshe Ben-Meir receives about 100 sacks of mail a day addressed to God. Moshe is the Director of Jerusalem's Dead Letter Office.

The New Age and Environmental Silliness

Remember the 1992 story about the man who received an organ transplant from a baboon? I cut that story out of the paper as I went on the air one day. I said, "I want to make a prediction. Some environmental crazies will show up at the hospital where this operation was performed protesting that the baboon never was asked to sign a consent form for the operation." The Crazies were there within hours. The baboon lovers epitomize much of that is wrong about the environmentalists of today. We humans have been assigned the task of Stewards of the earth, and we have failed in that task in many areas. The Al Gore led environmentalists of the '90s, are talking about much more than merely men and women taking care of our natural resources. They have elevated natural resources to the level of a deity, and demoted mankind, and more specifically industrial progress, to a role subordinate to nature.

Here are a few lines from an editorial written by Harvard Sociologist Professor Edward Wilson in an article titled *Is Humanity Suicidal?* in the May 30, 1993 issue of the New York Times magazine. Mr. Wilson wrote, "It was a misfortune . . . that a carnivorous primate and not some more benign form of animal made the breakthrough." The professor is apologizing for man's dominance over animals, and suggesting that maybe dolphins or squirrels could have been more noble masters of the Earth.

Many people point to Paul Ehrlich as the High Priest of Environmentalism today. They merely overlook the fact that Papa Paul's predictions of earth's endings about ten years ago didn't happen.

One of Mr. Ehrlich's main concerns is overpopulation. As we mention that subject we approach the real dichotomy of modern environmentalists. They suggest coercive abortion, the killing of the unborn in order to thin out humankind, while going to extreme lengths to protect any animal and the environment where that animal lives. Any lengths!

In California, homes have burned to the ground because their owners were forbidden by the environmentalists to clear away the scrub brush around their homes. The scrub brush, you see, was part of the environment protected so that the coyote could have a place to sleep in the shade and to urinate.

Weeks before the '92 Presidential Election Al Gore made a speech right in the middle of Las Cruces, New Mexico. I was driving through town that evening, and traffic was jammed. That is a disgrace, don't you think? Al Gore has said that the most destructive event in the history of mankind was the invention of the combustion engine. Now, all of those people who went to hear Al Gore drove to the event. If they were really environmentalists they would permanently park their cars. That, of course, would never happen. The environmentalists are out to harass and inconvenience other people, not themselves.

The environmentalists of today are connected to the New Age Religion. They pray to the Earth Goddess, and elevate animals to a level higher than mankind.

The New Age and Satanism

Hillary Clinton claims to have a special advisor in the White House, the ghost of Eleanor Roosevelt. Politically, this tracks. Eleanor was a strong supporter of the Communist Party, USA, a pal of many of the most radical left-wing movie stars and starlets, and as has been revealed in her personal letters, a Lesbian. I have no evidence that Hillary Clinton is herself a Lesbian, but she certainly likes to appoint them to high positions in her Government.

Is this "advisor" to Hillary Clinton actually Eleanor Roosevelt? The answer is "Who knows?" Any time the new agers contact a power source they are very possibly communicating with a very real spirit entity. The obvious problem is that the spirits have no way of documenting their identity, and could be spirits from anywhere, sent by anyone. They could, in fact, be demons sent by Satan himself.

Most scholars who have studied demonic possession know that demons need what many call "windows" to take over a human body. The demon needs what amounts to an invitation in order to invade a human body. Some of the more easily recognizable windows are games like Ouiga Boards, Dungeons and Dragons, Satanic Music, Satanic Rituals, and Drugs.

The New Age practice of Channeling, made popular by Shirley McClaine, is simply the opening up of oneself to spirits, allowing them to take over your mind and body for a while. I am convinced that Channeling does indeed give spirits access to our bodies. I am also convinced that this is one of the most dangerous things human beings can do. They casually lend their bodies to whatever spirit happens to be close when they issue the invitation. The same people who do Channeling wouldn't think of leaving the door to their homes open for anyone who wanted to stroll in and do whatever pleased them.

Hillary and her New Age friends ask the spirit world for whatever it has to offer. Some people will lose their minds, and their souls as a result of this casual experimentation.

The futility of entertaining unknown spirits really hits me when I visit a spirit-filled Christian Church. The Holy Ghost, God Almighty Himself, will certainly visit you, and fill you up with "The real thing." Why bother with the foolishness of poking your head into dark holes to see what you can bump into, and "enlighten" yourself? Why indeed, when the Holy Ghost is waiting right now, right this very instant, for you to invite Him into your life? If you really haven't experienced the power of the Holy Ghost, please start looking for it now. You will never be the same once you find Him.

Satanism And Drugs

One of the most powerful windows to involvement with Satanic Forces is provided by drugs. This is not a speculation or guess of mine. Across the country law enforcement officials are reporting increasing incidents of drug busts where drug paraphernalia and Satanic paraphernalia were found at the same place. Consider the infamous Matamoras Killings. Mass murders were committed by a group of drug dealers who actually believed that their human sacrifices to Satan bought them protection. Penitentiaries are packed with people who were fooled by that "promise" from Satan.

Two of the most *Politically Correct* drugs are Marijuana and LSD. It is the *Political Correctness*, the chic aura that has been assigned to these drugs that makes them so dangerous.

As a drug counselor with decades of experience I can assure you that Marijuana is one of the most destructive, and I mean destructive to the very core fabric of what a person is, drugs available. Marijuana is especially dangerous because of the persisting myth that it is non addictive, non harmful and that smoking it is a mark of sophistication. I wish you had been with me to hear the stories of all the wonderfully talented people who are now so brain dead that they merely exist, and all because of their addiction to Marijuana.

Let me first put the lie that Marijuana is not addictive into the closest septic tank where that lie belongs. Any action can become addictive. People are as surely addicted to watching TV, to reading Pornography, to smoking cigarettes and to eating chocolate as other people are addicted to cocaine and to heroine. There are millions of people in America tonight who would gladly stop smoking marijuana if they could.

One caller to my radio program clearly illustrated what marijuana does to the human brain. She told my call screener that she wanted to set me straight. She had just heard me say that Marijuana causes short term memory loss, and that she smoked marijuana, and because she made "C's" in school I was a liar. I took her call, and told her that after a two minute commercial we would continue our conversation. After the commercial she couldn't remember why she had called. I rest my case. America is filled with talented people who have literally burned their talent up in the smoke from Marijuana.

Marijuana smokers talk like they do for a reason. All of those "Like wow, man," and "Its like you know when," phrases are used so they can finish a sentence with a brain that has been, sometimes permanently, shifted into a lower gear.

LSD was blessed by writers of the '60s like Ken Kesey and Harvard Professor Timothy Leary. Ken Kesey wrote *One Flew Over the Cuckoo's Nest*, perhaps one of the best pieces of 20th Century American Literature. What has he written since then? I read one piece he wrote for Rolling Stone, and the first couple of paragraphs were so incoherent that I didn't finish the article.

Surgeon General Joycelyn Elders has suggested that we legalize drugs in America. Hours after she said that responsible legislators were calling for her resignation. Think about it, America. This woman's solutions to our problems are condom distribution and the legalization of drugs.

Other Invitations to Satan

If New Age Worship, Satanic Rituals and Drug Abuse are all potential windows to Satan, what other ways could he find into a human life? I am firmly convinced that anything you wear, listen to, read, watch on TV or in a Movie that resides on the fringes of Satanism serves as an invitation for Satan and other demonic forces to come into your life.

In detention centers and group homes for children where I have served as a supervisor, the first thing a child does on arrival, is to inventory with a staff member, all of their clothing, books, magazines, cassette tapes, everything they have. If they have a shirt with a picture of a demon on it, that shirt is locked up until they leave, and the same goes for anything that holds even a hint of demonism or satanic implication. The reason is simple. The children I deal with all have serious problems dealing with life on life's terms. Nothing related to Satan or to demonism will be permitted under my supervision, because those things have evil and negative meanings and messages that the child cannot use to their own good or for self-improvement. Be assured, taking these things away from children causes horrific reactions, because of the negative enmeshments the children have with those trappings of evil, and often with the dark forces behind those things.

For a more in depth appreciation of how absolutely everything we bring into our world influences us, I recommend Pastor Gary L. Greenwald's book, *Seduction Exposed*. In his introduction, Pastor Greenwald writes, ". . . anyone who brings an accursed object into his home or wears it on his body actually invites curses and evil spirits to oppress his life."

In recent years I have read about how psychologists have isolated so many factors that affect the way human beings behave. The Colors we surround ourselves with, the amount of light we have in our lives, the clothes we wear, the music and the words we hear, all contribute in a significant way to who we are.

We are primarily spiritual beings, who happen to have bodies and brains. I once heard a psychiatrist explain that you couldn't separate a mental experience from a physical experience because a thought is an electro-chemical process. You can no more distinguish the difference between the mental and the physical as you can distinguish between the physical and the spiritual. If our body is strong and healthy our spirit is free to soar, while if we are ill, our spirit tends also to weaken.

The grandest gift we humans can give ourselves is a cleansing of our spirits, through a cleansing of our environment. The medieval monks were taught to have custody of the eyes, a discipline over everything they choose to see. Custody of the eyes has never been as vital to spiritual health as it is in our high tech age of inter active media. We can chose to bring almost anything we choose into our life. Knowing that with each choice we also chose an alteration, either a growth or a marring of the spirit, leads us to surround ourselves with goodness. David said it in Psalms 101:3, *I will set before my eyes no vile thing.*

The Sound of Music

One of the most powerful stimuli for human beings is music. Choirs can lift their voices in concert for some of the most glorious praise that man can offer to God.

Music can also defile both man and his God. Today's children have access to some of the most foul language in the world, and it is marketed as music. Bob Demoss, from Focus On The Family, and his staff transcribed the words from an album by 2 Live Crew, *As Nasty As They Wanna Be*. He found that the "F" word was used 226 times, the act of oral sex was mentioned 87 times, women were referred to as B's or W's 63 times, and vulgar names for male and female genitalia were used 117 times. If you confront youth about what they put into their minds, via their ears, they will often respond, "I just listen to the music," or, "Its only words." Words are not now, and were never intended to be used as casually as if they had no meaning. In Mathew 12:36 we learn that *. . . men will have to give an account on the day of judgement for every careless word they have spoken. For by your words you will be acquitted, and by your words you will be condemned.*

Some people, especially the young, don't have treasure chests of positive stimulation and uplifting material in their homes. Some people become the trash they watch, listen to, sing about and read.

Rap Person Sister Souljah (sorry, but I am not about to call these people artists) once said that black people should take a week off from killing each other, and kill white people. Mr. Clinton, in his usual straight to the point style said, that maybe that was not a good thing to say. Mr. Clinton's former friend, The Reverend Jessie Jackson immediately attacked Mr. Clinton. (For what? For not wanting black people to kill white people?)

There are still some responsible people in the Music Industry. David Geffin, Chairman of Geffin Records said, "Its not a matter of censorship. Its a matter of responsibility. You can make money selling cocaine. I chose not to." When Geffin refused to distribute a Geto Boys Album that featured a song about the joys of necrophilia they found someone who would, Time Warner.

Consider the Source

Many Americans, both adult and children, spend two forty hour weeks. One forty hours is spent at work or at school, while the other is spent passively absorbing whatever programming the TV has to offer. A survey of the 104 top TV writers and executives reveals some of the motivation behind TV programming: This study was conducted by the Center for Media and Public Affairs.

	TV People	Real People
Believe Adultry Is Wrong	49%	85%
Have No Religious Affiliation	45%	4%
Believe Homosexual Acts Are Wrong	20%	76%
Believe In Abortion	97%	59%

Its Only Words

Haven't you heard "its only words!" enough? Just in case you aren't convinced of the total stupidity of that illogic, consider the two rap persons arrested in the same week for (You might have already guessed it) assault. They are not the only nationally recognized Gangster Rappers who have been indicted for assault and or murder.

Tupac Amaru Shakur, who had been interviewed on MTV with a pistol in his trousers, was arrested in Atlanta and charged with shooting two off duty police officers. By the way, this paragon of courage shot both men in the back.

The day after Shakur's arrest, a Rap Person named Flavor Flav was arrested for attempted murder. He was released on

$15,000 bail, and went immediately into treatment for crack addiction.

So much for the "Its only words" nonsense. Not only are their audiences acting out the words from their lyrics, but the rap people are now really shooting the people they always rap about shooting. Surprised?

The Cause

Keep in mind that the crusaders for *Political Correctness* are fighting in what they think of as a religious war, and they are quite serious about "The Cause." One zealot is Movie Director, Richard Donner, who directed Lethal Weapon 3. Here are some of the "messages" he sent to America:

- Murtaugh's (Danny Glover) daughter sports a T-Shirt that says, Pro Choice.
- A truck is forced off the road, with a sign that reads, "Only Animals Should Wear Fur."
- A sign on the Police Wall urges "Recycle."
- Riggs (Mel Gibson) drinks gas, and spits it out, saying, "Phew! Exxon." (Mr. Donner said, "Its our statement against Exxon.")

Mr. Donner said, "under the guise of entertainment you can sneak a lot of messages in. If one person gets interested then you've served The Cause."

All Time Low

If it makes someone a buck then it can be sold. Right? Consider this marketing effort from a pusher of child pornography. These lines were in a sales flyer he sent to potential customers. I received the flyer in a letter from the Concerned Women for America who want to stop Attorney General Janet Reno from protecting this sort of sleaze. The flyer read, in part, Our latest, and completely legal video of teen and pre-teen girls, ages 12–16 is ready right now, and its called "Sassy Sylphs."

This really makes me sad to be an American, and I thought I'd never say words like that. When our government protects the human debris who pedal that sort of thing, and don't champion their victims, America is in very serious trouble.

The Washington Solution?

In this chapter I have reported thus far on things people use as a substitute for, or as a diversion away from God. One of the most available false Gods for Americans is their government. In 1992 many Americans were totally caught up in the presidential election, many of them actually believing that the right president could and would fix America, and make it all better just like Mommie used to do. Take a closer look at our government, and consider the futility of waiting on Uncle Sam.

Our President, a man who was elected on a slogan of "Character isn't an issue," and has never had a job, is, according to Ross Perot, unqualified for middle management, and was closer to the KGB than he was to the ROTC during "His War." He doesn't run the government anyway.

The government is run by a New Ager who had herself blessed by a Shaman prior to discussion of Health Care, but excluded any real Physicians from the planning. Her "Advisor" happens to be the last known Lesbian first lady, Eleanor Roosevelt, who just happens to be dead. Our Attorney General wants more protection for the freedom of speech child pornographers. Our Surgeon General sounds like a recording embedded in a condom dispenser who makes occasional weird pronouncements like "We should legalize drugs." Our former Secretary of Defense allowed U.S. Army Rangers to die because he didn't want to offend anyone politically by sending Armored Support to Somalia.

Martin L. Gross wrote an exposé on government waste titled *A Call For Revolution.* If it weren't so heartbreaking it would be high comedy. Mr. Gross reminds us of James Madison's warning. We were told that if we didn't remain vigilant our government could become overcentralized and turn into an oligarchy run by selfish politicians in Washington. He illustrates an America gone berserk with hundreds of examples. Here are two;

- The city of Anchorage, Alaska was threatened with stiff fines by the federal government if they didn't decrease pollution in its waste water, even though there was no need to decrease pollution. To comply with the government's bullying they spent $428 million to pollute and then to clean up their water.
- If our government wrote checks for $14,700 to all 7.7 million of our poor families, it would cost only $113 million a year, compared to the $300 million we spend annually on welfare.

Many people, even though they are painfully aware of how inept the government is, long for free government health care. Wake up and smell the paper mill, America! Don't look now, but the VA is our best example of free government health care. The last time I visited a VA Hospital I met a man with a sleeping bag, who said that he had given up waiting for treatment in the past, and was determined to wait until he was treated. Medicaid, meanwhile, has been exposed repeatedly as one of the most corrupt operations in the world. Doctors are notorious for using Medicaid money to take trips to the Super Bowl or to stock their wine cellars. We know all of this. Its nothing new, yet we wait with eager anticipation for our government to simply take over the most complicated industry in America, and make it all better.

The Spreading Tentacles

The Clinton government appears to operate on a very flaky premise. The premise is:

The more incompetence we demonstrate the more responsibility we demand.

Mr. Clinton promised repeatedly not to raise taxes. He said:
- "We should cut middle class taxes immediately by ten percent" Mr. Clinton (September, 1992).
- "We want to give modest middle-class tax relief to . . . families with incomes of under $60,000 per year." Mr. Clinton in the first debate (October, 1992).
- "I will slash boondoggle projects." Mr. Clinton, *Putting People First.*

In his book, Rush Limbaugh devotes an entire Chapter titled Lies, Lies to the lies Mr. Clinton has told the American people. They are many, and they are becoming legion.

While we are told that the government is sizing down it continues to swell. The Clinton Health Care Plan offers great insight into how government can invade the lives of the American people.

The first announcement that I remember being released from Hillary Clinton's secret talks on health care was that abortion would be part of the funded package. That is a violation of existing laws so what, surmises Hillary and her Health Care Planning team. America wants Health Care so badly they'll give up some things, perhaps many things in order to have "Free" health care.

Have you noticed, that before anything has actually been settled related to the pending Health Care Plan just how far the tentacles of Health Care have gone, in an invasion of human rights and decency in our country? Did you ever suspect that health care would include such other areas as:
- Gun control (People will shoot each other with guns, and being killed is bad for your Health. Therefore gun control is suddenly a Health Care problem.)
- Education (AIDS and teen pregnancy are health related, and to solve those problems the government plans to marry Planned Parenthood to the National Education

Association, and teach children the Politically Correct
way to be Healthy.)

- Health Care might as well include the services of the IRS,
the CIA, the FBI, the Department of the Interior. (As soon
as the government can get all of the information on you
on those little health care cards, then that one card can
be used by virtually all government agencies. Did you
notice that the Health Care Card was already designed,
and in Mr. Clinton's hand the night he began talking
about Health Care?)

The government that demonstrated that it couldn't even administer the House Bank without disastrous consequence
wants to take over the control of everything we do. It is, considering the track record of the government, a lousy idea.

Big Bang Boondoggle

Last summer, on the day the funding for the Super Collider
was being voted on in Washington I was driving from Dallas to
Houston. I was listening to the Larry King radio program. Larry
was interviewing some scientist who had written a book about
the Super Collider. He said that he was going to explain, in
terms everyone could understand, why the Super Collider was
so important. He began his explanation with something like this.

The earth began with a Big Bang. We already know what
happened during most of that first second after the bang. The
Super Collider will help us to discover what happened in the first
fourteen to twenty one hundredths of that second.

I felt so informed. I thought those folks in Texas were just
dumping money down a big hole. I really had no idea that they
were trying to disprove the biblical account of creation. Those
fellas are trying to recreate the big bang, an event that never
happened in the first place.

This is a Fact!

Mr. Bill Clinton and Hillary, are not going to drop by your house tonight to talk about your problems. They are very probably going to continue to initiate foolishness that will actually exacerbate your problems. They aren't going to solve them. So who does that leave?

Dan Quayle Was Right

Mr. Quayle said that a return to family values was needed in America. Can you guess why the left reacted like screaming banshees to that simple suggestion? They reacted because they knew that he had hit upon the truth, and that the truth threatened the maintenance of the value erosion they had engineered for the past thirty years.

Mr. Quayle concluded that speech, made infamous by a liberal media, with these profound words. He said: " . . . the time has come to renew our public commitment to our judeo-christian values. . . . We are, as our children recite each morning, 'one nation under God'. That's a useful framework for acknowledging a duty and an authority higher than our own pleasures and personal ambitions."

The primary family value of a nation under God is the maintenance of family under God. When families, led by Fathers who set examples of Manly Christian behavior, and Loving and devoted mothers once again become an American standard, then our children will again have a place to turn away from violence and institutionalized stupidity. The first step in taking back our streets is taking back our living rooms. The unbridled hedonism of today is boring and without meaning compared to a loving membership in a God-Centered family.

Families, real families living life based on God's teachings, work so well for one simple reason. Their design is divine. A man and a woman, joined in a sacramental bond, devoted to each other and to their children can beat the odds in this age of ungodliness. Families do more than hold answers to our problems, they are the answers.

The song, titled God Bless America, is a brief and profound prayer. If enough people say it often enough it will be answered. The logical compliment to that three word prayer is understood:

God Bless America—and please begin with my family.

Chapter 11

Champs and Chumps

If John Madden can have his very own all pro team, then I can name my own All Star Champions of both *Political Correctness* and *Political Incorrectness.* This chapter will be brief, and one of the most entertaining to write. I'll start with our team.

Marvin's Champions of Political Incorrectness
The Good Guys

1. **Congressman Bob Dornan** from California. This man is a political "brawler." He read hours and hours of Special Orders on C-Span exposing the cowardly behavior, or misbehavior, of Bill Clinton during the Vietnam years. He also went to Somalia, and brought back the very personal biographies of the Rangers who gave their lives in that country because of political ineptness. His tribute was as grand a National Eulogy as has ever been delivered. A patriot, a leader, a broadcaster who substitutes for Rush Limbaugh, a man with a steel trap for a mind, and as obviously a man of presidential timber as this old priest has ever seen.

2. **Former Secretary of Education, William Bennett.** This man can take any warped and misconstrued issue, and unravel the *Politically Correct* facade from the truth as well as any man in America today. His eloquence and succinctness of speech lead him to the heart of matters. Another man who would sit extremely well in the Oval Office.

3. **Former Vice President and his wife, Dan and Marilyn Quayle**. They took the heat, when America played the very ugly "dump on Danny" game. They both championed family values, and showed America what a great family could do if they ignored the press. I sang "Danny Boy," opening my program as a tribute to these All Stars of Political Incorrectness.

4. **Rush Limbaugh.** This man reminds me of the advice my high school football coach always gave us concerning how to be a great football player. The coach used to recite, "Evah Day! Evah Day! Evah Day!" Rush booms out the truth to America, and he does it, Evah Day, Evah Day, Evah Day.

5. **Barry Farber.** Not as well known a broadcaster as Rush, but just as powerful. He is an older man, epitomizing what I always think of as a Southern Gentleman. Barry represents a part of America I regard as sacred, a charming yet fiery member of an older generation, patiently teaching America, often through simple stories of his own daily life, how grand it really is to be an American.

6. **Pat Robertson.** The Christian equivalent of Rush Limbaugh. He reports the news of the day from the perspective of a Christian. Pat Robertson's 700 Club represents the most concise and accurate source of news reporting, unbiased by political Correctness, in America today.

7. **James Dobson of Focus on The Family.** The name of the organization led by this Psychologist-Broadcaster tells it all. Dr. Dobson has said that he never intended to be a watchdog against Politically Correct activity in this country. Because of Focus on The Family, the day may soon arrive when people like Dr. Dobson return their attention

to solving people problems. Meanwhile, we need more Champions like Dr. Dobson.

8. **Michael Medved** is a movie critic who exposed his own profession for the preponderance of sloop they were selling to the American Public. It has made a difference.You and I can talk about how crude and inappropriate Hollywood has been, but when one of their own courageously blows the whistle on their foolishness it gets their attention. What American so badly needs are Michael Medveds in virtually every walk of life. It will happen.

9. **Bill Cosby** can do an hour of great comedy without mentioning off-color things or using any of the other crutches the unfunny people use to generate laughter. The man is as funny now as he was thirty years ago.

10. **Warren Moon,** a quarterback, a leader, a Christian gentleman, a class act. A highlight of my year always occurs on those days when I watch this professional at work. His behavior off the field is as classy as what he does on the field. Here is an athlete who is much more than well paid, but is blessed in his ministry to underprivileged youth. He consistently puts back into the community that supports him. Warren also says that an athlete does indeed have a responsibility to serve as a role model for youth.

Now for the other team, those well paid perpetrators of the putrid, the solicitors of slime, the ambassadors of trash, the *Politically Correct* all star team.

Marvin's Politically Correct All Stars

1. **Phil Donahue** is without equal in this category, and therefore deserving of the position of team Captain. I offer these two samples of Phil's work from his TV shows; Phil entertained a group of former employees of Pan American Airlines. A handsome, young Captain stood up and told, with great passion, of how Flight 103

had been blown out of the sky by Lybian Terrorists, and effectively closed down the airline, all because the planes, with American Flags on their tails had been symbols of America. Phil went ballistic and berated the Captain, comparing the bombing of Flight 103 to President Reagan's Air Raid directed at Colonel Quadaffi. On a more recent show, Phil entertained the cast of this year's TV offering of smut, NYPD Blue. On his show were people who opposed the program, and when he talked to them he ridiculed their objections with silly voices and degrading comments.

2. **Sally Jesse Raphael** is close behind Donahue. She made a presentation of an award to Rush Limbaugh, admitting him into the Radio Broadcaster's Hall Of Fame, and insulted him at the same time. The next week one of her shows illustrated the "Style" she consistently presents to the American Public. Sally did a show on Mothers and Daughters who have sex with the same men.

3. **Axle Rose,** the lead "singer" of Guns and Roses deserves an award. In 1993, during the Christmas season, Axel and his group released an album, that featured a song written in prison by Charles Manson. One announcer said that it was okay for Axel to do this because he was going to donate the profits to one of Charles' victims. Forget who gets paid, America, wonder as well as yours truly, what Charles Manson could have to say to make our country a better place. How many children will listen to Axle singing Manson instead of something worthwhile.

4. **Madonna** belongs in this lineup. Posters in New York City subways featured Madonna alongside Mary, the Mother of God, and asked people to make a choice. Madonna has run naked through the streets, literally pushing her obscenity into the faces, or up against

the windshields, of people who didn't ask for it.
Madonna is a "crusader for filth."

5. **Dr. Ruth Westheimer** deserves a spot on this team
simply because the Team Captain, Phil Donahue,
publicly acknowledged her as Politically Correct. Here
is a physician who has the attention of millions of
people, and could do great things to stop teen
pregnancies and slow the spread of AIDS. Instead
of helping to solve problems she persists in spreading
them, advising youth to use brightly colored, maybe
even glow in the dark condoms.

6. **Joycelyn Elders,** Surgeon General of the United
States. The only good thing I can find about this
woman is that everything she says illustrates the poor
taste of Mr. Bill Clinton who appointed her. She wants
to distribute condoms to children who are too young
to use them and to solve the problem of prison
overcrowding by legalizing drugs.

7. **Ross Perot.** This man has done some good things
for America, but they are all overshadowed by the
fact that he is the man most responsible for the
election of Bill Clinton. His disciples will inevitably
say that he didn't know that he couldn't win the
election. Think about it. Here is a brilliant billionaire,
who carried out a vendetta against George Bush,
giving the presidency of the United States to a man
Mr. Perot has said was not qualified for middle
management. Ross Perot knew exactly what he was
doing, and, like everything else he has ever done, he
had his own selfish reason for doing it.

8. **The Reverend Jessie Jackson** is included here
because of the way his message has degenerated
as he sold his political soul for Political Correctness.
This is a man whose words I used to thrill to, because
they were the words of personal responsibility, of hope,
and self reliance. The same man who led thousands

to understand their worth as human beings in the '60s is now justifying violence. Jessie Jackson teaches what I think of as the new math; Poverty, plus oppression, equal violence. (Jessie, you have so many people who will follow anywhere you lead, and you have an opportunity today to lead those people away from the hopelessness of victimhood, toward hope based on personal responsibility. I pray for you often because we need you back on the right side.)

9. **Time Warner, Inc.,** wins this special group award. This is Corporate America at its worst. Time Warner, Inc. is so focused on the bottom line (Profits) that they have total disregard for what they distribute to the American people. They have packaged and marketed the regurgitation of societies' human debris, selling everything from Madonna's pornographic book *Sex,* to the *Gangster Rap* songs that are most assuredly contributing to the violence in America today.

10. **MTV,** a video network, is one of the most powerful political arms of Liberalism in America today. This network openly and unabashedly campaigned for Bill Clinton, and celebrated his election, proclaiming that "one of us" is now in the White House. Meanwhile, they claim that their programming doesn't really cause violence. They laughingly claim that Beavis and B—head are nothing more than a joke. (Don't look now, MTV, but Beavis and B—head, thanks to you, are rapidly becoming your audience.)

God help us all!

Chapter 12

Conclusion

What can we do to enlighten people to the evils of *Political Correctness?* I believe we should educate them to the *deceit* of Political Correctness. Then explain the alternatives to this ideology by being guided by God's law in a Christ-centered family.

America has been under the dark cloak of Political Correctness for so many decades that many families do not know how to be "God-centered." For this reason, I urge those who desire to improve their families to go "back-to-basics"—the Christian values set up by our founding fathers. You may affirm this commitment by making the following pledge:

> I beseech You, Almighty God,
> to grant me the blessing of God the Father,
> the love of his only Son, Jesus Christ and,
> the discernment and power of the Holy Ghost,
> to enable me to keep this sacred promise.
> I pledge to wear no garment, T-shirt, cap or
> other apparel that depicts or glorifies Satan,
> demons or sinful behavior or depicts or glorifies
> any person who glorifies those things.
> I will keep my home as I would keep your temple—
> free from certainTV programs, tapes, magazines,
> books, music, or anything else that offends you.
> I promise to take full responsibility for the role you
> have assigned me in my family, and I will join my
> family each day for prayer.
> I will attend no event that offends you.

I will join and participate in the activities of a
Christian church.
Grant me the strength to keep this pledge and bring
me closer to You, Precious Lord.
Amen.

Other Books by Starburst Publishers

(Partial listing—full list available on request)

Political Correctness Exposed   —Marvin Sprouse

Subtitled—*A Piranha in Your Bathtub.* Explores the history of Political Correctness, how it originated, who keeps it alive today, and more importantly, how to combat Political Correctness. Contains 25 of the most frequently-told Politically Correct lies.

(trade paper) ISBN 0914984624   **$9.95**

Angels, Angels, Angels   —Phil Phillips

Subtitled—*Embraced by The Light...or...Embraced by The Darkness?* Discovering the truth about Angels, Near-Death Experiences and other Spiritual Awakenings. Also, why the sudden interest in angels in this day and age? Can we trust what we read in books like *Embraced By The Light?*

(trade paper) ISBN 0914984659   **$10.95**

Dinosaurs, The Bible, Barney & Beyond   —Phil Phillips

In-depth look at Evolution, Creation Science, and Dinosaurs in the media and toys. Reader learns why Barney, the oversized purple dinosaur, has become a pal to millions of children, and what kind of role model is Barney.

(trade paper) ISBN 0914984594   **$9.95**

Turmoil In The Toy Box   —Phil Phillips

A shocking exposé of the toy and cartoon industry—unmasks the New Age, Occult, Violent, and Satanic influences that have invaded the once innocent toy box. Over 175,000 in print.

(trade paper) ISBN 0914984047   **$9.95**

Turmoil In The Toy Box II   —Joan Hake Robie

This book takes a hard look at the popular "Nintendo" games, the "Batman" craze, "Ghostbusters," "Freddy" from *A Nightmare on Elm Street,* Dungeons and Dragons and much more. Seeks to make every parent aware of the potential for mental, emotional and spiritual harm from allowing their children access to toys and TV that will give them more of a foundation in the occult than in God's teaching.

(trade paper) ISBN 0914984209   **$9.95**
(audio cassette) ISBN 0914984268   **$7.95**

Books by Starburst Publishers—cont'd.

The Truth About Dungeons & Dragons —Joan Hake Robie

A close look at the fascinating yet dangerous game of Dungeons and Dragons. What it is about. Why it holds such fascination for certain people, especially young, well-educated and gifted people.

(trade paper) ISBN 0914984373 **$5.95**
(audio cassette) ISBN 091498425X **$7.95**

Teenage Mutant Ninja Turtles Exposed! —Joan Hake Robie

Looks closely at the national popularity of Teenage Mutant Ninja Turtles. Tells what they teach and how this "turtle" philosophy affects children (and adults) mentally, emotionally, socially, morally, and spiritually. The book gives the answer to what we can do about the problem.

(trade paper) ISBN 0914984314 **$5.95**

Halloween And Satanism —Phil Phillips and Joan Hake Robie

This book traces the origins of Halloween and gives the true meaning behind this celebration of "fun and games." Jack-O-Lanterns, Cats, Bats, and Ghosts are much more than costumes and window decorations. In this book you will discover that involvement in any form of the occult will bring you more than "good fortune." It will lead you deeper and deeper into the Satanic realm, which ultimately leads to death. Over 90,000 in print.

(trade paper) ISBN 091498411X **$9.95**

Horror And Violence—The Deadly Duo In The Media —Phil Phillips and Joan Hake Robie

Americans are hooked on violence! Muggings, kidnappings, rape and murders are commonplace via your TV set. This book not only brings you up-to-date on what is happening in the media in general, but also will help you and your children survive with integrity in a complex media environment.

(trade paper) ISBN 0914984160 **$9.95**

Reverse The Curse In Your Life —Joan Hake Robie

A handy "guidebook" for those who wish to avoid Satan's snares. Includes Biblical Curses, Forbidden Practices, Warfare Prayers, and much more. This book is the result of author Joan Hake Robie's over ten years of research on the subject of the occult, demons, and Satanism.

(trade paper) ISBN 0914984241 **$7.95**

TemperaMysticism
—Shirley Ann Miller

Subtitled—*Exploding The Temperament Theory*. Former Astrologer reveals how Christians (including some well-respected leaders) are being lured into the occult by practicing the Temperaments (Sanguine, Choleric, Phlegmatic, and Melancholy) and other New Age personality typologies.

(trade paper) ISBN 0914984306 **$8.95**

Beyond The River
—Gilbert Morris & Bobby Funderburk

The first novel of *The Far Fields* series, **Beyond the River** makes for intriguing reading with high spiritual warfare impact. Set in the future and in the mode of *Brave New World* and *1984*, **Beyond The River** presents a world that is ruined by modern social and spiritual trends. This anti-utopian novel offers an excellent opportunity to speak to the issues of the New Age and "politically-correct" doctrines that are sweeping the country.

(trade paper) ISBN 0914984519 **$8.95**

The World's Oldest Health Plan
—Kathleen O'Bannon Baldinger

Subtitled: *Health, Nutrition and Healing from the Bible*. Offers a complete health plan for body, mind and spirit, just as Jesus did. It includes programs for diet, exercise and mental health. Contains foods and recipes to lower cholesterol and blood pressure, improve the immune system and other bodily functions, reduce stress, reduce or cure constipation, eliminate insomnia, reduce forgetfulness, confusion and anger, increase circulation and thinking ability, eliminate "yeast" problems, improve digestion, and much more.

(trade paper-opens flat) ISBN 0914984578 **$14.95**

Purchasing Information

Listed books are available from your favorite Bookstore, either from current stock or special order. To assist bookstore in locating your selection be sure to give title, author, and ISBN #. If unable to purchase from the bookstore you may order direct from STARBURST PUBLISHERS. When ordering enclose full payment plus $2.50* for shipping and handling ($3.00* if Canada or Overseas). Payment in US Funds only. Please allow two to three weeks minimum (longer overseas) for delivery. Make checks payable to and mail to STARBURST PUBLISHERS, P.O. Box 4123, LANCASTER, PA 17604. **Prices subject to change without notice.** Catalog available upon request.

*We reserve the right to ship your order the least expensive way. If you desire first class (domestic) or air shipment (Canada) please enclose shipping funds as follows: First Class within the USA enclose $4.50, Airmail Canada enclose $6.00.   10-94